Praise for *Pivot*

"Whether you are reclaiming your optimal health, reinventing yourself, or rediscovering your passions and joy, *Pivot* is the perfect book to catapult you into the next stratosphere of your life and new possibility. Markel has done a brilliant job of converging all of his wisdom and genius into a magnificent body of work that we all can benefit from. Simply a MUST-read."

> —Lisa Nichols, author of the *New York Times* bestseller *No Matter What!,* and CEO of Motivating the Masses, Inc.

"In *Pivot*, Markel has created a road map for honoring the ordinary life by finding one's extraordinary gifts. I was inspired to more courageously embrace my own reinvention story and trust that I'm on the right track—even when it doesn't feel that way."

> —Karen Leland, author of *The Brand Mapping Strategy*

"With the extraordinary information and practical focus of *Pivot*, this is a must-read for anyone who is reinventing their life—or even thinking about it! Adam has made the reinvention process simple!"

> —Jill Lublin, three-time bestselling author, international speaker, and radical influence expert

"Pivot in your life, pivot in your body and your business. This book will show you how. It all starts with the first step."

> —Bob Proctor, author of *You Were Born Rich*

"Pivot over to the bookstore and let Markel show you how just a tiny change in your thinking will create a massive transformation in your career and life."

> —Phil Town, financial adviser and author of the number one *New York Times* bestseller *Rule #1*

PIVOT

The Art and Science of Reinventing Your Life

ADAM MARKEL

ATRIA BOOKS

NEW YORK   LONDON   TORONTO   SYDNEY   NEW DELHI

ATRIA BOOKS
An Imprint of Simon & Schuster, Inc.
1230 Avenue of the Americas
New York, NY 10020

First Atria Books hardcover edition April 2016

ATRIA B O O K S and colophon are trademarks of Simon & Schuster, Inc.

For information about special discounts for bulk purchases, please contact Simon & Schuster Special Sales at 1-866-506-1949 or business@simonandschuster.com.

The Simon & Schuster Speakers Bureau can bring authors to your live event. For more information or to book an event, contact the Simon & Schuster Speakers Bureau at 1-866-248-3049 or visit our website at www.simonspeakers.com.

Interior design by Kyoko Watanabe

Manufactured in the United States of America

10 9 8 7 6 5 4 3 2 1

Library of Congress Cataloging-in-Publication Data

Markel, Adam.
  Pivot : tapping into your full potential / Adam Markel.—First Edition.
    pages cm
  Summary: "A practical and inspirational program for reinventing yourself, whether you are out of work or want to change your professional trajectory"—Provided by publisher.
  Includes bibliographical references and index.
  1. Self-actualization (Psychology) I. Title.
  BF637.S4M3556 2016
  158.1—dc23   2015029937

ISBN 978-1-4767-7947-8
ISBN 978-1-4767-7949-2 (ebook)

158.1
M

This book is dedicated to my loving wife, Randi, who has always believed in me unconditionally; our amazing children Chelsea, Lindsay, Max, and Eden, who inspired this book to be a reference guide for their life's journey; and my real-brother, Keith, and my parents, Irene and Kenneth, who gave me freedom to express my own voice.

CONTENTS

INTRODUCTION:
THE LIFEBOAT

Begin by knowing that you have already arrived.

—RICHARD BACH, AUTHOR

IMAGINE . . .

You're on a cruise ship, one of the largest in the world. You're traveling from exotic port to exotic port, enjoying fine dining, dancing, and every luxury.

And then the unthinkable happens.

One night, you're startled awake in your cabin to the harsh clang of alarms. You can hear doors slamming, loud voices in the passageway outside. A fist pounds against your door. "Get out now!" a voice shouts.

You stand up from your bed, then lose your balance and fall right back down again—the floor is sloping away, and you realize . . .

The ship is sinking.

You scramble into your clothes and rush into the passage, and are immediately swept along by a tide of panicking passengers. You fight to stay upright and eventually make it to an emergency exit and up to the upper deck.

Sometime later, you find yourself floating in a small lifeboat with four other people. There is no land in sight. No sign of your ship, its crew, or any other passengers.

You take stock of supplies and scan the horizon for hours. Nothing.

Eventually you settle into your new reality. The five of you hunker down in the raft and do what people always do when there is nothing else to do: You talk.

You share a little about who you are. Your work. Your skills. Your family. What excites you. Your hopes and dreams for home.

Time moves on. What began, you were sure, as a short wait for rescue has turned into three days at sea. With no end in sight.

◆

A scenario much like this one kicks off the New Peaks "Life Directions" training program that I teach. It's called the Lifeboat Game.

As the game proceeds, the participants get a new set of instructions: There are enough supplies on the boat for only two people to survive at sea.

You must now make your case for why you should be one of the two people to be saved.

Many participants speak from their hearts and share who they are and why they are a valuable asset to their families, their friends, their business associates, and the world. Just as many speak from their heads, making logical arguments about their abilities and why they should be saved.

Some participants sacrifice themselves by giving up their seats to others on the boat. They do this because they believe someone else has more to offer the world, or they feel their sacrifice is an act of greater value or that they have already lived a rich and full life.

Eventually the participants are given the painful task of deciding who will stay and who must die, and they must explain why they voted as they did.

What starts as a game quickly becomes a powerful emotional experience. It's not uncommon for participants to raise their voices and for emotions such as anger, resentment, and hurt to come to the surface.

It's not uncommon, in fact, for people to begin to cry as a new, perhaps previously unrealized emotion rises within them: regret. The sudden, unexpected reality that they're not living the life they hoped they would, or knew they could, can be a shattering experience.

Because if there's one thing the Lifeboat Game is good for, it's revealing when something is fundamentally wrong with your life.

◆

You're not in a lifeboat at sea right now, but I suspect you've picked up this book for a very similar reason: Something is wrong.

You might know what that "something" is. Your work, your health, your relationship, and your business are all pretty safe bets.

But there's an equally good chance you don't know what's wrong. You can't articulate what the problem is. But you can feel it.

Can't you?

I know, because I've been there. By my late thirties, I could definitely feel that something was wrong.

I was living a successful life by most standards. I'd been married for seventeen years to the love of my life. We had four beautiful children. I'd built a successful law practice and was enjoying all the perks that came with it. Sure, I was working seventy to eighty hours a week in my law firm, occasionally even sleeping in the office, but I was making bags of money and life was good.

But something was wrong.

I would wake up in the morning with a sense of dread about the day. I started losing my hair, and my body began to change in ways that I didn't like. Once a fit, healthy athlete, I was losing energy and vitality almost by the day.

Worse, though, was the increasing sense that something was missing. Even though I was earning great money, I was unhappy with the daily grind. I was always working. And every day it seemed as though my soul was shriveling. Some part of me, some spark, some purpose, was dying on the vine.

I couldn't quite put my finger on it, but I began to believe, for the first time, that my life was not my own.

I started to wonder: *Is this all there is?*

I wasn't nursing the hurt of missing out on a dream of being a rock star or an athlete or an animal trainer or a missionary. I didn't know what I wanted or what I was missing. I just knew I was missing something.

By picking up this book, I know you feel it, too. Maybe, like many people, you can't quite identify what the problem is. You don't quite understand why a little voice keeps telling you something's not right here.

So you ignore it. You put your head down, and you do what you think you have to: You show up. Day after day you show up, and you do what you think you should.

But the voice doesn't go away. Not entirely. You're still left with a sense that you're not on the path you dreamed of. That you could do more. Have more. *Be more.*

Yes, at times you can quiet the voice. You take a vacation or buy something shiny. And it works, for a while. So you try to ignore the truth a little longer. You watch endless hours of television. You drink. Eat.

And it works. For a while. Maybe you get married. You buy a nicer home. You get a promotion. Life is okay. For a while.

But eventually the cracks begin to show. Maybe it's that extra thirty or forty pounds you're carrying. Maybe it's the relationship challenges. Or lack of relationships. Perhaps it's the near-constant fatigue or the health complaints that don't seem to go away like they used to.

Maybe it's the sense of dread you feel when your alarm goes off and the lack of energy and enthusiasm you feel for life. Maybe it's anger—often for no reason you can identify.

Maybe it's all of those things and more. But whatever it looks like for you, the voice is the same: *Something's not right here.*

If this is what it feels like for you—if you feel that something's wrong, or that your life is slowly filling with unexplained anger, or exhaustion, or hopelessness—then know this: *Those rising feelings will eventually drown you if you keep ignoring them.*

You can try to ignore them, but you will fail. You can try to explain away these feelings, but you will fail. Because right now, in this very moment, you are tolerating your own slow, agonizing death.

And it's time to change.

The Wake-up Call

Despite the obvious cracks in my life and the ever-present voice telling me to admit to having problems, I did what most people do: I ignored them. I hushed the voice, I put my head down, and I kept going. After all, there were bills to pay. Clients to see.

I needed a wake-up call, and, naturally, I got one.

My call came on a clear October day in New Jersey. I was driving with my wife, Randi, when a feeling overcame me: *I need to stop this car*.

I pulled over and asked my wife to drive.

We switched seats. "Do you need to make a call?" she asked.

"Just make a left up here, honey. I'll tell you what's going on."

What was going on was that I was having pain in my chest. Randi's face paled, but she followed my directions until we arrived at the medical center not far from our home in Freehold, New Jersey.

We pulled up to the emergency entrance, and the next thing I remember is sitting in a wheelchair with wires running to my chest. My hands tingled. I was in a cold sweat as I struggled to fight off the waves of dizziness that left me veering between the edges of vomiting and passing out.

All I could think was: *I'm going to die today. I'm never going to see the kids again.*

My mind, like my heart, was racing. I couldn't stop thinking that I had never become the person I expected to be. I wasn't the father or husband I had planned and promised myself I would be. I was a slave to my eighty-hour-a-week job, and this—*this*—was how it would all end.

I cursed under my breath and thought, *I'm not even forty, for crying out loud.*

And now I was going to die.

The only thing more palpable than my fear was my deep sense of remorse. I had screwed it up. I had had one chance, and I had wasted it so carelessly that I could scarcely believe my own stupidity. In what seemed like the blink of an eye, I'd gone from being an idealistic teenager and dream-filled twentysomething to a cynical middle-aged lawyer.

I'd gone from the prime of life to being a small, scared, shivering man in a hospital gown, wondering, *What happened?*

Later, when a man in surgical garb appeared at my bedside, I was so filled with regret that I could barely speak. I simply waited for him to deliver my sentence.

"Mr. Markel," he said, "you're not going to die."

I almost cried. The words sent a wave of relief through me so deep that it's difficult to describe.

I realized that the doctor was still talking.

"I asked how many cups of coffee you've had today."

"I'm a lawyer," I replied, "and I've only had five or six cups so far today."

The doctor held back his laughter. "You were lucky—this time. You're experiencing an anxiety attack brought on by too much caffeine and too much stress."

Both my wife and I began to cry.

His tone turned more serious. "You need to lay off the coffee," he said, "and you need to take a look at where your life is headed. You might not be as fortunate next time."

I left the hospital that day holding my wife's hand. As we walked outside, I looked up to the sky, and without thinking I simply said, "Thank you. Thank you, God."

Up to that point in my life, I had been anything but religious. I was open to the idea of spirituality, but I'd never spoken a word to God that I could recall. But in that moment I felt I'd been given a reprieve, a second chance to make real my dreams of creating a meaningful life. I felt such overwhelming gratitude that I had to thank *someone*.

As we drove away, I made a vow: I would not go back to living the same way. I would not lie down again on the job of living a life that meant something.

At that moment I had no idea what to do. But I knew I had to do something.

That "something" was to reinvent my life.

◆

And that's what I did. Now, less than a decade later, I'm CEO of and partner in one of the largest training companies in the world. I speak to thousands of people each year in my role as a transformational trainer. And although my hair never did grow back, we left our old life and routines in New Jersey and moved to a beautiful community in California. I still appreciate my roots in the East Coast, but here there's no snow and I can surf instead of shovel.

What matters, though, is that the voice is quiet. Rather than tolerate my old life any longer, I chose to reinvent it.

I chose to *pivot*.

Pivot: The Art and Science of Reinventing Your Career and Life

I love basketball.

Not just for the athletics or the competition. Not just for the speed, rhythm, and finesse, either. Those are all great reasons to enjoy the sport, but I love it all the more for how it mirrors real life. Like life, basketball is a team sport. You play with others and drive toward a goal. Things can change quickly, but preparation and persistence almost always pay off. Like life, it's a game of ups and downs, talent and drive, hard work and big rewards.

It's also a game of momentum. In basketball, players have to dribble while moving with the ball. You can't just hold the ball and run down the court—you have to bounce the ball between your hand and the floor. If you stop dribbling, you have to stop moving—you can't make any more progress toward the goal.

It's a great metaphor for life. You need to stay engaged—keep dribbling—or you lose your momentum. You stop making progress.

But in basketball, as in life, there are always options. A player who has stopped dribbling can still pass the ball. He can shoot. And he can *pivot*.

To pivot means to plant one foot and rotate on it while holding the ball. That simple move lets you turn 360 degrees to see the entire court and the players while keeping control of the ball—in other words, it allows you to protect yourself while still exploring your options for moving the game forward.

Pivoting is a key strategy in basketball, and it's even more essential in life. Faced with a lack of momentum, who doesn't want to protect themselves while exploring the options for moving ahead? It's the perfect word for the process of reinventing yourself in midgame.

The word *pivot* has other uses, too, and they're just as enticing:

- In your body, a pivot joint, like the one in your neck, lets a joint rotate without falling apart or breaking.
- In physics, a pivot is a critical part of gaining leverage— doing more with less.
- In business, a pivot is a change of strategy to capture more market share, or surmount a difficult obstacle, without failing.

These definitions all have something in common. They're all ways of taking a less advantageous circumstance and making it better.

Imagine if, like a basketball player, you could get a complete view of your life so you could improve your chances of winning without giving up the ball. Imagine if, like a lever, you could do far more with the energy you're expending now. What if, like a neck joint, you could change directions without doing damage? Or, like a start-up company, you could try a new strategy to overcome an obstacle?

That's what it means to pivot.

In life, as in basketball, it's an option you can choose at any time. I wrote this book to teach you how.

What's Your Pivot?

For me, pivoting meant reinventing myself as someone who was no longer on the destructive treadmill of a legal career. For you, reinvention might be something very different. Your pivot might mean:

- Starting the business you always dreamed of.
- Recovering from illness or rediscovering the health you once had.
- Finding a new career or reaching new heights in your current one.
- Changing your life to allow for more time for your passions and your loved ones.
- Discovering a new relationship.
- Rediscovering a lost or long-buried passion from your past.

Whatever your pivot might be, the goal is the same: to reinvent the parts of your life that aren't working, so that you can live a life that brings you fulfillment. Whether your pivot is in your work, your relationships, your health, or your personal passions, *Pivot* is a toolkit and road map for reinventing your life—and doing it *without* destroying everything you've built so far.

What to Expect from *Pivot*

As you learn the strategies of *Pivot*, you'll meet many others who have used these tools to reinvent themselves, such as:

- Barbara Niven, who was a single mother in Portland, Oregon, and became a Hollywood actress.
- Dennis Kolb, who was diagnosed with leukemia and faced survival odds of 0.01 percent. He's now the CEO

of a foundation helping those facing life-threatening diagnoses.

- Dr. Venus Opal Reese, who was homeless and eating out of trash cans at the age of sixteen. Now an entrepreneur and speaker, she holds four degrees, has been featured on ABC, CBS, PBS, and many other media outlets, and has consulted for O: *The Oprah Magazine.*
- Lisa Lent, who transformed herself from flight attendant to million-dollar CEO.
- Joe Gebbia, who, along with his roommate, Brian Chesky, built the billion-dollar company Airbnb from three air mattresses on the floor of their apartment.

There are many more stories to come and thousands more out there in the world. Every person's story is different, but they all share a common thread of reinventing themselves using a process that worked for them, and will work for you. It's a process that will give you:

- **A road map to follow.** Pivoting is a process. It's a journey from where you are now to somewhere new. The best journeys need a map.
- **Inspiration.** Success leaves clues, as they say, and pivoting is no exception. You'll gather inspiration—fuel for your journey—and insight from the stories of others who've done it.
- **Realism.** This book may stretch you, but it won't ignore reality. Pivoting is about building a plan that works for you and your life—it's not about abandoning your responsibilities or leaping from a cliff.
- **Tools for change.** *Pivot* is about working on yourself and your life, and it's hard to work without tools. You'll find plenty of exercises, insights, and tips to help you make sustainable change.

Whether you want to reinvent your career or reinvigorate your relationships, *Pivot* can help you.

Fifty Pages of Your Life

I don't believe in accidents. I believe everything happens for a reason.

You might feel differently. And that's fine. You don't have to believe in fate in order to pivot.

But consider this: You're reading a book right now about *how to transform your life.*

Why?

How did you find it? Did the cover catch your eye? Did a friend give it to you? Did you read the summary or flip through the pages, and something resonated?

For some reason, you're holding it in your hands. You can call it random chance. Or you can believe in something larger—that's up to you. But the fact remains: Whether you believe you found the book or the book found you, *it's yours.*

And I think that's something to take seriously.

If you're like most people, though, you read fifty pages of a book like this and move on. The book sits on your shelf. It collects dust on your bedside table. It lies neglected in the archives of your e-book reader. It goes on to an illustrious career as a stand for your computer monitor.

It's time for that to change.

Why? Because when you read fifty pages and move on, you're not just giving up on a book; you're giving up on *yourself.*

You may not realize it, but your fifty-page habit is rearing its head elsewhere. What else are you "fifty-paging" in your life? Are you fifty-paging your relationship? Your parenting? Your health? Your finances? If you're only going two chapters deep in your life, you're only going to get two-chapter results. And take it from me, two chapters gets you only as far as the emergency room. It doesn't always get you out.

"Fifty-page syndrome" is just another way of saying *quitting*. Don't do it.

You want to pivot? You want to change your life? It starts with *not quitting*. Quitting is the number one success killer. You're not going to fail because you ran out of money or the economy changed or you were too busy or, or, or—you'll fail only if you quit.

So stop quitting.

Commit to finishing this book. Hey, you've already bought it. My sales pitch is long over. I have no vested interest in you finishing the book beyond the fact that *if you fifty-page this book, you're going to keep fifty-paging your life*.

And it's not going to work.

It's time to stop just showing up. It's time to commit. Read the book. Make the plan. Work the plan.

That's how you pivot.

How This Book Is Structured

Every pivot shares two things. Whether it's losing a hundred pounds, starting a business, getting a dream job, or sailing around the world, every pivot story has two parts. Two changes, if you will.

Neither is optional.

Your pivot requires these two things, just as the pivots you're going to read about did, too. The requirements are that you change *what you believe* and *how you behave*. This book is divided into two parts, based on those two things.

PART I: Clarity: Changing Your Pivot Beliefs

Every pivot begins with changing what you believe. No, you don't have to take on a new faith or abandon an old one. But you do have to change the way you think. The first part of this book is focused on that shift, and it's mainly an internal one. It's the "inside job" of pivoting, and its goal is to reach clarity about what it is that you want and to deal with the mental and emotional obstacles that will stop you from getting there. You'll challenge pivot myths, learn to face fear, and get clear about what it is you *really* want.

PART II: Momentum: Creating Your Pivot Behaviors

Of course, as necessary as belief is, it's only part of the job. You can believe all you want, but you'll need to take action. The second half of the book shifts to your "external" pivot. You'll begin to change your behaviors with a goal of building momentum in your pivot. Like a snowball gathering size or an engine coming to life, building momentum helps you move steadily ahead, recover from setbacks, and deal with the practical challenges of transforming your life. In this section you'll build a plan to pivot and take your first steps toward your new life.

Throughout those two parts of the book, you'll find Pivot Points: key takeaways within each chapter. They're clearly identified in the text and summarized at the end of each chapter. If you need to refresh your memory or your motivation, refer back to those summarized Pivot Points at any time.

You'll also find Pivotal Questions at the end of each chapter. These are meant to prompt you to look more closely at your own life in the context of the pivot process. I encourage you to use a journal to explore your answers to these questions. It's not required—this isn't school, and there's no homework. But after helping many thousands of people, I can testify that there's a deeper level of understanding to be found through the act of writing.

At the end of the book, you'll find a twenty-one-day action plan. It takes the elements of the book and arranges them in a series of daily actions that you can take to find clarity and build momentum.

You don't need to be special to pivot. You don't need to be any richer, smarter, or more advantaged than you already are. In the pages that follow, you'll discover the stories and strategies used by other people just like you. You'll discover a lot about yourself and about how you tick. And you'll begin to take the real-world steps that will transform your life.

The tools you'll learn to use in this book are intended to instruct you and inspire you. And they're designed to help you take action—because in life, as in basketball, when you stand still, you're toast. You have to pivot to survive and win.

Using the principles in this book, I went from being an eighty-hour-a-week workaholic lawyer to having my dream job as a transformational trainer and CEO of one of the most respected personal and business success training companies in the world. I went from being so far off purpose that I thought I was dying to being completely centered and whole.

And I'm not alone.

I've personally witnessed the breakthrough transformations of people from more than one hundred countries around the world. In the past two decades, our company has trained more than a million people. I know you can pivot because I've seen it happen—over and over again, to people just like you. People with the same circumstances (or worse), the same financial barriers (or worse), the same physical limitations (or worse). I've seen a lot of change, and I know anyone is capable of pivoting.

There's only one rule: *Don't be that fifty-page person.*

Don't phone it in. Don't give in to apathy or fear. Because everything changes when you pivot, and I don't want you to miss it.

Don't wait. You don't have to wait for the "moment." The crash. The heart attack. The divorce. The cancer, the bankruptcy, the depression. You don't have to wait.

My wake-up call made me realize that my very soul was shriveling up. I was dying from the inside out. My trip to the hospital was the reality check that I was tolerating mediocrity. I was putting up with the status quo. Worse yet, I was *supporting* it. I was putting all my energy into preserving a life that was killing me.

Are you doing the same?

If so, how long are you willing to tolerate it?

Because you don't have to. You don't have to put up with the status quo. You don't have to tolerate the way things are. You can change. You can reinvent yourself.

You can *pivot*.

PART I

CLARITY

Changing Your
Pivot Beliefs

This then is the real key to life: *if you change your mind, your conditions must change too.*

—Emmet Fox

The Windshield:
An Introduction to Clarity

RIGHT NOW, you're blind and you don't know it.

It's a selective blindness that only affects your ability to see yourself. You can't see just how unhappy you've become. How far your health or your relationships or your enthusiasm have fallen. That's why you know something's wrong but you can't articulate it: Your ability to clearly see your life is severely compromised.

Worse still, not only can you not see yourself in the present, but you can't see the future, either. You've lost the ability to dream about days and years to come, to envision a life that's different from the one you lead now, and to feel that sense of possibility that we all felt at one time in our lives.

You are, in effect, functionally blind.

Sure, you can still get around, do your job, and fulfill your responsibilities—in fact, you've probably become a master of "getting by." But it's as if you're trying to do it while staring at the world through a dirty windshield. Your vision is so narrow and compromised that you're relying on habits, memories, and sheer dumb luck to get you from A to B.

Over time, our experiences—the millions of moments that pass through our lives—change the way we see things. Our relationships, our emotions, the impressions of our childhood—all leave behind traces. They build up like dirt on a windshield, and they change how we see the world and, in turn, how we navigate through it.

Your parents' attitudes about money and the work they did changed your windshield, adding a layer through which you try to see the world.

Your most emotionally charged moments—the good and the bad—have tinted your vision.

Your daily habits limit the scope of your vision, narrowing it from the wide-open gaze of youth to the tunnel vision of the daily grind.

The people you spend your time with. The culture you grew up in. The books you read, the things you study, the content you watch—everything adds to the windshield.

A news article adds a speck here.

A comment from a friend adds a smear there.

A bankruptcy throws a wave of mud.

A betrayal leaves a layer of silt.

We try to clear those things away—we try to shake them off, hold to our own vision, make our own decisions. But no one gets through clean. The great gift—and the great curse—of life is that it changes you. And over time you begin to see the world differently.

You still catch glimpses of the "real" world through the tiny clear areas left on your windshield, but as you push ahead, you see less reality and more a view of the world that's distorted, blurred, and obstructed by the grime of life.

Most of these changes happen over time, beneath the level of conscious awareness—"life windshields" get dirty over decades, a gradual buildup that happens so slowly we don't even realize it. Just as you don't notice that your arteries are half clogged or that your weight is drifting up, the loss of clarity is so subtle you have no idea it's even happening.

But it is. And it has a profound impact on your life.

The dirtier your windshield becomes, the more you tend to run on autopilot. You rely on regular routines and habits to get through the day. Up to 45 percent of our daily actions are habitual—we do them without any conscious thought. We get up at the same time. Eat the same thing. Drive the same routes. Do our work the same way. The result is that we live our lives almost completely unconsciously. Although we don't realize it, we're not actually thinking about what it is that we do or what it is that we want.

When your vision is blurred, it's difficult to get your bearings. You lose your sense of direction. The distant dreams and goals you once had become indistinct and eventually disappear from view. You may try occasionally to get reoriented, but by the time you realize that you've lost your way, you can't even tell which direction you're driving anymore. You are, in effect, lost.

Finally, at some point, you simply stop moving altogether. Like a basketball player who's stopped dribbling, you're no longer making any progress.

The first and most important challenge of your pivot is to clear your vision and rediscover clarity.

The first part of this book is about clearing the windshield of life. It's about removing the grime and dirt, polishing the scratches, and sealing the cracks left behind by a lifetime of . . . well, life . . . so that, perhaps for the first time, you can really see.

Because once you can see clearly, you can decide where you want to go and just go there.

Sure, it may be a long drive. There may be unexpected detours and breakdowns. But as long as you keep clearing the windshield— keep reaching for clarity—you can keep driving.

Because the one thing I've learned in working with thousands of people is this: *No clarity, no pivot.*

Getting Clear: Six Steps to Clarity

No clarity, no pivot. That's our mantra for Part I of this book and for the six chapters that follow. *You need to reach a new level of clarity before you can create a new type of life.*

▶● PIVOT POINT: You need to reach a new level of clarity before
you can create a new type of life.

But how can you get there? How can you clear your windshield
and find clarity?

There are six steps on the path to clarity. Think of each one as
a way of removing another layer of vision-limiting grime on your
windshield. In the following chapters, we'll travel those six steps and
tackle the obstacles to clarity head-on.

> **Chapter 1: Un-believe.** Most people can't even take the
> smallest of steps toward a new life because they believe
> they can't. Your first stop on the road to clarity is to un-
> believe the myths that are keeping you stuck right where
> you are.
> **Chapter 2: Let Go.** To move past where you are now, you
> need to be able to release past hurts and detach from the
> need to know exactly how your pivot will unfold.
> **Chapter 3: Face Your Fear.** Pivoting requires you to leave
> your comfort zone. To do that, you'll have to tackle your
> fear. You don't have to eliminate fear to pivot, but you do
> have to be able to take action in the face of it.
> **Chapter 4: Enter the Pivot Phone Booth.** Changing your life
> means changing *yourself*. For that, you need the seeds of a
> new identity. You're going to enter the pivot phone booth
> as Clark Kent and emerge as not a new you but the *real*
> you.
> **Chapter 5: Envision Your Future: Finding Your Life's
> Purpose.** Even a clear windshield won't help if you don't
> know where you're going. In this chapter, you'll develop a
> clear vision for your new direction and the life you want.
> **Chapter 6: Big-D Decide.** This is the goal of Part I of *Pivot*:
> to reach a "Big-D" decision—a commitment to take action
> that's so powerful that you simply *must* take action.

Knowing Clarity When You See It

If I've done my job right, by the end of these six chapters you'll have a very different view of your past, your current life, and your choices for the path ahead. You'll become so clear and so committed that the next steps—the actual act of pivoting toward your new life—become simple. They may not be easy, but they will be clear.

Most important, the idea of pivoting is going to feel much different. With true clarity you'll find that:

- **You have a feeling of confidence and possibility.** Things will seem "obvious." You'll find a new confidence in making the shifts toward your new life and a sense that more things seem possible than ever before.
- **Fear moves to the background.** I won't promise you that it will vanish—although it might—but most people discover that the fears holding them back are no longer in control.
- **You have more energy.** Your energy level will improve dramatically, and you will discover new capabilities and resources within you and around you that you never knew existed.
- **Your mood is better.** Clarity has a tendency to make you feel happier. The people around you may notice it before you do, but rest assured it's there.

Be forewarned: Those things combined may make you feel very different indeed. In fact, they're likely to release a sensation you may not have felt in a long time. It's called *hope*.

With clarity, the path ahead becomes clear. It becomes so obvious, so inspiring, and so empowering that taking action (see Part II) will transform your goals from something you could never do into something you *must*.

So let's get started.

1

Un-believe

Remember, you can have anything you want if you will give up the belief that you can't have it.

—DR. ROBERT ANTHONY, AUTHOR

A QUICK question: What do you think the purpose of this book is?

It's a simple question, and I ask a similar one at seminars around the world: What's the purpose of our time here today?

So what is it? After all, I know *why* you picked up this book—it's because something is wrong. Now I want to know how you think this book will help. What's its purpose? What do you expect from it?

If you're like most first-time participants in one of our training events (the veterans know better), your answer will likely be: To learn something. It's a natural response—most people think that the purpose of a book or a seminar is to learn something. To gain knowledge.

Well, most people are wrong.

The vast majority of what happens in great seminars, and in great books, is unlearning. Those *aha!* moments you feel in a great training program or during a particularly enlightening passage of a book? They don't happen because you learned something. They happen because you *un*learned—that flash of insight was realizing that something you thought you knew just wasn't true.

I'm not talking about unlearning facts. Discovering that a tomato is a fruit and not a vegetable won't change your life much. The unlearning that matters for your pivot is much deeper. It's not about changing your knowledge.

It's about changing your beliefs.

Facing the Truth

When I was working as a full-time attorney, profoundly unhappy with my life, I began reading books like the one in your hands right now.

The most fundamental shift in my life happened not when I began to lead transformational training programs or head a company that was aligned with my heart but when those books helped me stop believing things that weren't true.

I had always believed that the "American dream" was my ticket to fulfillment. I believed that if I put my head down and worked hard at any well-paying profession, I would be happy.

Yet there I was, living the American dream—and miserable.

When I faced the reality that my beliefs weren't serving me and were in fact hurting me, it was impossible for me to reconcile the paradox. I could no longer believe that the path I was on would lead to happiness, when it so clearly did not. I simply couldn't believe what I believed any longer.

Faced with that truth, I became unsure of my earlier choices, and I began to truly consider the prospect of pivoting seriously. That moment of "un-believing" is where my journey actually began. And it's where yours will, too.

You Are What You Believe

To appreciate how profoundly your beliefs affect your life—in fact, to accept that your beliefs *create* your life—it may be easier to begin with a phenomenon that we've all experienced: the placebo effect.

The placebo effect is a benefit we get from a medical treatment that doesn't actually have any active medicinal substance. A sugar pill for a headache, for example, will often give pain relief. Fake surgeries can outperform some real ones in providing relief, for instance, from knee pain. Just seeing the Apple logo sparks more creative thinking.

The placebo effect is a remarkable thing, and new research shows that we can get benefits even when we know something is a placebo.

Think about that for a moment: I can give you a sugar pill, and I can tell you it's a sugar pill, but as long as you believe it will work, there's a decent chance that it will. And by *work*, I mean that taking that sugar pill will create almost the exact same neurochemical changes in your brain that a real aspirin does. Your body's biochemistry is changing because you expect it to. Your pain is going away *because you believe it will*.

Despite decades of study, we still don't really have a good grasp of how the placebo effect works. But there's no denying that it does. It's real, scientifically accepted evidence that *what you believe has the power to change your reality*.

New and Old Beliefs

If a belief can take away pain or deliver the same results as surgery, what else can it do? Knowing that beliefs create your reality gives you a whole new starting point for beginning to pivot, and that is to stop believing things that don't serve your reinvention.

Our first step in that process is to drag those limiting beliefs—the pain-inducing, life-limiting myths you might believe—out into the light and expose them for what they are.

The tricky thing about beliefs, though, is that it's often difficult to even realize we have them. We've been conditioned over time to accept things without ever consciously deciding, *This is what I believe to be true.*

For example, right now you may think:

Entrepreneurs are extroverted.
I have my mother's hips.
Once you're past fifty, it's too late to start again.

These are all beliefs. They're things that many people choose to accept as fact, but guess what? They aren't facts. Lots of entrepreneurs are introverts. There's a mountain of evidence that your genes are not your destiny. And plenty of people reinvent themselves after age fifty. I see it happen all the time.

But, true or not, beliefs can become self-fulfilling prophecies. And that means that everything that is part of your life is there because a belief has supported its existence. A person in an abusive relationship may believe that she is not worthy of love or that he deserves to be punished for reasons going back to childhood. A person who loses money may believe that rich and successful people are greedy or unhappy. A person who works at a job or business she dislikes may believe that she doesn't have the talent or time or money to be successful in another career.

But beliefs aren't facts. They're a choice. You get to pick the ones you want. Why choose ones that don't serve you?

◆

Before we look at instilling new beliefs—a process you'll go through during the 21-Day Pivot Plan at the end of Part II of this book— there's enormous value in taking an inventory of the things that are consciously or unconsciously holding you in place. And although everyone's life is unique, there are some limiting beliefs that are common to many pivots.

For the six myths that follow, consider how each might be affecting you. You don't need to "fix" them. You can begin by realizing that beliefs are nothing more than conditioned thoughts you have received through the influential people and experiences in your life.

Myth No. 1: Pivoting is for other people.

I have witnessed more personal transformations than most people will see in a thousand lifetimes. It's one of the most profound gifts of my own pivot: I now get to watch as people reinvent themselves and *come alive*.

Of the millions of people who live with the mediocrity of their routines or jobs every day, most back away from facing it. I am fortunate enough to work with people who, instead of retreating, chose to do something.

Guess what's special about each of them?

Nothing.

That's right. Nothing.

Without exception, the multitude of pivots I have witnessed are executed by people who are just plain normal. They're not freakishly lucky, intelligent, or beautiful. They're not Ivy League, upper-class, or megarich. They're just . . . normal. They're so normal that their stories would be boring but for the fact that they have transformed themselves so dramatically.

Plenty of people with less time, money, charm, and savvy than you have pivoted. Like you, they had "normal" lives, and they chose to reinvent themselves. Were they scared to pivot? Yes. Did they have financial challenges? Yes. Time pressures? Yes. Kids, mortgages, careers, car payments, and more? Yes! But they did it anyway, and so can you.

And therein lies the simple secret of reinvention: Those who pivot aren't extraordinary. They *become* extraordinary when they decide they will not tolerate the circumstances of their lives for one moment longer.

Does that mean that your obstacles aren't real? No—broke is broke, a mortgage is a real contract, and your kids are yours (even if there are days when you might wish differently). You don't need to pretend that your bills aren't real.

You do, however, need to stop pretending that you aren't good enough.

Let go of the idea that living the life you want is for someone else. Someone richer, smarter, more talented, or luckier. It's nonsense. Pivoting isn't a privilege, a genetic windfall, or a birthright.

Pivoting is a choice.

▶● PIVOT POINT: You don't have to be special to pivot. You become special when you decide to.

Becoming extraordinary isn't a pivot requirement; it's a *result*.

Myth No. 2: It's too risky.

My visit to the emergency room was an incredible stroke of good luck. Many other pivoters have had similar experiences—they've experienced an epiphany that has changed the course of their future. For some, it was a car accident; for others, an illness.

But many have not been so lucky. For every person who has a brush with death and wakes up to change her life, there are many who don't wake up at all.

Maybe you haven't had your own "ER moment." Maybe the heart attack or the divorce or the breakdown hasn't happened.

Don't wait for it.

If you're telling yourself that pivoting is too risky, be sure you understand the real risk. Be sure, before we go any further, that you understand the stakes. Because this isn't about "Wouldn't it be nice if . . ." This is about watching the life you could have had get further and further away, until it's so far gone you can no longer see it.

This is about regret. And there is nothing more painful.

Those are the stakes, and they're real.

Did your stomach just drop? It should have. This is your life we're talking about. But that's the best part. It's your life. You get to change it.

What you're feeling is normal. That voice urging you to start anew is normal. The myriad signs and conversations and ideas that happen too often to be coincidental—all of that is normal, too. Because the stakes are high. The real risk is in not changing.

You have a chance for a different life. You can have a "second act" in life. Hell, you can have a third, fourth, or fifth act! Have as many as you want.

Have as many as you need. Because that's the truth about pivoting. You don't just want to. You don't just get to. You *need* to. Because what's the alternative? Staring into the abyss between you and what you once dreamed you could be? The bitter taste of regret? It's just not an option.

Do you have any idea what's at risk?

▶• PIVOT POINT: The real risk of change isn't that you might try and fail. It's that you might not try and you'll regret it.

Myth No. 3: You have to burn the ships.

Some five hundred years ago, when Hernán Cortés reached the shores of what is now known as Mexico, he faced some very real, very serious obstacles. Conquerors had attempted to colonize the Yucatán before and failed. Cortés, who had only six hundred men and had never actually led anyone in battle before, was behind before he even started, and there was already talk of mutiny. With the odds stacked against him and his men's morale ebbing, Cortés destroyed his fleet of ships.

"Burning the ships" is what economists call a "commitment device"—a way of overcoming our short-term desires in favor of longer-term ones. When you have money automatically deducted from your paycheck or bank account for retirement, you're using a commitment device to overcome your short-term desire to spend, for your own long-term good.

Today we don't really burn or sink ships in a literal sense, but the idea is still with us. Poker stars go "all in" in the hope of crushing an opponent. Athletes give "110 percent." Entrepreneurs "put it all on the line" or "bet the farm." We "go out on a limb," because it's "all or nothing."

It's a pervasive, and persuasive, idea. Over and over we're told that in order to succeed, we have to (a) take enormous risks and (b) commit completely to our dreams by abandoning our old lives. The idea is reinforced by books, movies, stories, documentaries, and news coverage of people who "risked it all" for fame, fortune, and love.

The trouble is that the idea is nonsense.

It's not that the stories we hear aren't true, it's that they tend to be outliers—the rare "daring-risk" successes that make for great Holly-wood tales. In fact, the vast majority of happy, successful people got there by gradually working toward their goals. If poker were the best way to get rich, casinos would be out of business.

Still, the myth is a compelling one—we love the rags-to-riches storyline. But the danger of the myth isn't that it leads us toward the gambling risk of "all or nothing." The real danger of the burn-the-boats myth is that it gives us an excuse to stay put. After all, what re-sponsible person would risk everything for a dream? The myth gives you permission to stay right where you are because you're "doing the right thing." You're keeping the food in your kids' mouths. You're keeping a roof over your heads. To pursue your dream? To pivot? Why, that would be just plain irresponsible.

And there's the trap.

In fact, pivoting isn't about sudden radical change. It's about:

- Envisioning a realistic way to change your life
- Preserving the parts of your life that serve you
- Creating a clear plan for making sustainable change

Pivoting is not an extreme sport. It's a real way for real people to change their lives. To view it any other way isn't part of pivoting—that's just unnecessary risk.

When I decided I needed to leave the practice of law, and find and follow my true purpose, I didn't stop being a lawyer the next day. I had a family. A mortgage. Bills to pay. I had responsibilities to staff and clients. To ignore all that and burn the ships would have been disastrous.

Instead, I started exploring what I called my "Purpose-Driven Plan B." I began to gradually create a bridge from Plan A—the practice of law that I was currently doing—to Plan B, which was to help people find and follow their true purpose.

As that bridge strengthened and grew, I gradually began to dismantle Plan A. I reduced my commitments over time to my clients as I began to grow and learn and develop my skill in Plan B.

Eventually? Plan B *became* Plan A. No burning of ships or betting of farms required.

The burn-the-boats fallacy might be the most devastating myth because it's the one that keeps the most people trapped. Are you convinced that you have to quit your secure job to pivot? Spend your life savings? Abandon your friends or family? If you believe those things, pivoting seems impossible. How can you allow yourself to think clearly about changing your life if you feel that you have to risk everything? The answer is that you can't. As long as you believe that pivoting requires taking extraordinary risks, you'll never take action.

▶● PIVOT POINT: **Pivoting is not an extreme sport. It's a step-by-step, realistic way to change your life.**

Later in the book we'll look at when using commitment devices in larger quantities is useful, and how best to do it.

For now, know that the either-or decision is a false choice. You don't have to give up everything you have *now* in order to move toward what you want *tomorrow*.

Myth No. 4: What I want is unreasonable.

It's easy to think that your desire to pivot is frivolous. Unacceptable.
You might have been raised to think that dreams were just that—
dreams. You might have been told "Life is supposed to be hard" or
"Not everyone can have their dream job." If the people around you
are unhappy with their lives, you may feel that your desire to change
your life is somehow frivolous or unethical. That it's too much to
ask. That it's *wrong*.

It's not.

Want to know what *is* wrong? I'll tell you: slowly dying from the
inside out. That's wrong.

Teaching your kids, by example, to live in mediocrity? Wrong.

Wasting the life that you've been given by being unhappy? Also
wrong.

Yes, most people are unfulfilled. A Harris Interactive Survey
found that 55 percent of the workforce is hoping to change careers.
Eighty percent of people are not working in their "dream" job.

If you're unhappy with your job, your relationships, your health,
or your finances, you're not only not alone, you're part of the herd.
You're packed into a crowd bigger than a thousand Super Bowls.

Because most people aren't content. That's the real state of the
union.

But that's not the problem. It's sad that most people are unfulfilled. But that pales in comparison to the tragedy that *you* are unfulfilled and you think that it's somehow okay. That it's unreasonable
for you to want more than you have.

That is not reasonable. Not at all.

▶● PIVOT POINT: It's not wanting change that is unreasonable. It's
    tolerating unnecessary misery.

Myth No. 5: Everything I've done
so far will be wasted.

Many people are afraid to pivot because a voice inside them says, "This invalidates everything you've done."

Changing careers doesn't make your previous career a waste. A new relationship doesn't mean your last decade was wasted. Starting a business doesn't mean your 401(k) is lost or that the twenty years you spent on the corporate ladder were a waste.

Why?

First, you've learned a lot. You may not believe it, but that uninspiring decade you spent at your desk wasn't without purpose. You might not realize it, but you have skills, self-knowledge, and experience that are going to serve your pivot. There's a good chance that what you learned while you were unhappy is going to keep you from being unhappy again.

Second, pivots require a frame of reference. You can't pivot to something better if you've never been somewhere worse. You need the reference point of the poor health, the lousy job, the bad relationship, the abandoned dream, in order to know what you're leaving behind. Whatever it is that you've done so far in life—the good and the bad—is setting you up to be able to both pivot and appreciate it. Because a pivot without gratitude? That's just jumping from the frying pan into the fire.

Finally, your past is a clue to where you should be. As you'll discover later, all of the experiences and incidents in your life so far are clues to what you are truly committed to.

The past is never wasted. *Pivot* is about making sure you don't waste your future.

There's a name for our tendency to worry about how much we've invested in something: the sunk-cost fallacy. Whether it's a job, a home renovation, or a business investment, we hate the thought of walking away from something we've put time, money, or effort into, so we keep investing in those things, even when it no longer makes sense.

But the sunk-cost fallacy is just that—a fallacy. It's an irrational argument. Only, in this case, your focus on the past isn't just causing you to spend more on that bathroom renovation than you should, it's keeping you stuck in the life you have.

▶• PIVOT POINT: The past is never wasted. Pivoting is about making sure you don't waste your *future*.

Myth No. 6: I have to wait for . . .

Everyone on the planet has fallen for this myth at one time or another.

Once the kids leave home, I'll start a business.
As soon as spring comes, I'll start exercising.
Once it slows down at work, I'll have some time to start
    painting.

They all share one thing in common: They're variations on *someday*: *Someday I'll write a book. Run a marathon. See Italy.*

And what do we know about *someday*? It never comes. Years later the book isn't written. The college degree you always wanted isn't any closer. The furniture-making business is still just a few dusty tools hanging in the garage.

In fact, even our well-loved (and chronically unkept) New Year's resolutions are just a variation on the same theme. "I'm going to start working out on January first." How many times have you heard (or said) that? And how well does it work? Even when we disguise *someday* by giving it a date, it doesn't work.

This myth is about believing that you need to wait. For some thing, some day, some person, some event, some *sum*.

You don't. Waiting is the antithesis of pivoting.

Oh, I know why you're waiting. You want change to be clear, easy, and risk-free. Unfortunately, change often isn't any of these. But it can be easier than you think. The risk can be low. The steps can be small. The price can be affordable. But it can't wait.

Do you have to pack it all in and fly to Italy tomorrow? Of course not. Pivoting is a process. And you get to control that process. You don't have to quit your job or fly to Italy tomorrow. You can pivot in the smallest baby steps, over whatever time period you want.

But you cannot—must not—wait.

▶• PIVOT POINT: Waiting to change is the same as not changing at all.

I Can't, Because . . .

Any one of the six myths is an obstacle to achieving clarity and beginning your pivot. Each is a barrier to clarity.

Which ones do you need to un-believe?

Pretend for a moment that this is the last page of the book. Based on what you know now, you need to begin your pivot *tomorrow*. Imagine, for example, that you need to begin to become an entrepreneur tomorrow morning.

At this point, you're likely to feel some resistance. *But,* you think, *I can't start tomorrow because I have to go to work.*

Did you hear that?

You're hearing your false belief at work—the belief that pivoting is an either-or, zero-sum game. That you can't follow Path B unless you abandon Path A. Many people—including those in this book—became entrepreneurs without quitting their day jobs.

The problem is that our beliefs are really habits. They are patterns of thinking that we follow without, well, thinking. The vast majority of our lives is run by these types of habits, and until we drag them out into the light where we can see them for what they are (things that aren't true), our lives run on autopilot. We go about our lives believing the same things, day after day, and nothing changes.

Think about your pivot and about the idea of change. What is the first barrier that comes to mind? Fill in the blank below.

I can't start tomorrow because . . .

There it is. You just dragged it out into the light, kicking and screaming.

Now put that one aside. Whatever your answer was—your day job, your spouse, your finances, your kids, your pension, your job security, your bills—set it aside.

Now ask the question again.

And again.

When nothing else comes up? Those are your limiting beliefs.

Suspend Your Disbelief

Your beliefs weren't formed overnight. And erasing them may not happen overnight, either. It can take time, particularly for your most emotionally charged beliefs.

So, in the meantime, suspend them. Open your mind to the possibility that what you believe might not be true. After all, what do you have to lose?

It costs nothing to believe that reinventing your life is possible.

It costs nothing to believe that things can change.

It costs nothing to believe that *you are enough*.

What do you have to lose by believing something different?

►•PIVOT POINTS

- ➤ You don't have to be special to pivot. You become special when you decide to.

- ➤ The real risk of change isn't that you might try and fail. It's that you might not try and you'll regret it.

- ➤ Pivoting is not an extreme sport. It's a step-by-step, realistic way to change your life.

- ➤ It's not wanting change that is unreasonable. It's tolerating unnecessary misery.

- ➤ The past is never wasted. Pivoting is about making sure you don't waste your future.

- ➤ Waiting to change is the same as not changing at all.

▶•PIVOTAL QUESTIONS

1. What do I currently believe that might be preventing me from pivoting?

2. What would I have to believe to take a baby step toward my dream now?

3. What would I have to/need to believe about myself to be successful in my dream?

4. What would I have to believe about how others would support me in making my dream a reality?

2

Let Go

Some of us think holding on makes us strong; but sometimes it is letting go.

—HERMANN HESSE

WHEN I was eight years old, my mother arranged for me to spend
the summer with a friend of hers who lived in Los Angeles. Her
friend had two sons about my age, and when I arrived I was thrilled
to discover that we had a lot in common, including collecting baseball cards. Of course, they collected the Dodgers and Giants and I
collected the Mets and Yankees, but I quickly forgave them for their
poor judgment and we became fast friends.

As soon as I could get my mom on the phone, I pleaded with her
to send my own cards from New York. For a week I waited every
day at the mailbox for them to arrive, but there was no sign of my
beloved collection.

One day I was sitting with one of the boys and looking through
his cards when I noticed that he had many of the same cards that
I did—a lot of Yankees players for a western fan. Looking closer, I
noticed that, like me, he even had a much-sought-after Willie Mays

card. It was from 1973, Willie's last major-league season playing for the New York Mets. That card was the pinnacle of my collection and my most prized possession.

As soon as I saw the card in his hand, I had a visceral, painful reaction in my body. I knew something was wrong. I asked my mom's friend whether my mother had sent my cards and she said, "Yes, your mom sent baseball cards as a gift for my sons in appreciation for taking care of you."

I was devastated, inconsolable. I tried calling my mother, but the line was busy. After several tries, I simply lost it and ran to my room to scream and cry. I was heartbroken and felt deeply betrayed.

Sometime later, my mom's friend knocked on the door and asked to talk. She said that she'd spoken to my mother. She showed me the big envelope the cards came in. "It was addressed to me," she said. "See? It was a mistake, but we can fix it."

She took the envelope and told her sons to fill it as full as they could with cards and those would be mine. They did as she asked, and my collection was restored—with the exception of Willie Mays.

I was only eight, but I was profoundly hurt. I barely spoke the rest of the time that I was in Los Angeles. When I returned home, I refused to talk to my mom. She tried to explain, but I didn't want to hear anything she had to say. I felt I had been horribly betrayed.

I carried that incident with me for many years. Time and again I revisited the image of my prized card in my friend's hands. I wondered over and over why my mother had done what she had. Over and over I felt the hurt of betrayal and the anger of injustice.

And in that vicious cycle I learned my lesson well: *No one can be trusted.*

Tethered to the Past, Blocked by the Future

The destructive cycle of revisiting past hurts isn't just the purview of eight-year-olds. Many, if not most, adults carry the pain of the past with them. After all, no one gets through life unscathed. Who hasn't been hurt?

What most of us don't realize, though, is how destructive it is to revisit those painful moments over and over, without end. It would be years before I would learn the price of my inability to let go and forgive my mother (and others), and more time still before I finally did let go as part of my own pivot.

Now, with the clarity of hindsight, I know that not only was I forcing myself to feel the same negative emotions repeatedly, but I was deeply attached to them. They held, as we'll see, a strange power—just as the ones you feel do when you reflect on your own painful experiences.

That type of attachment is the second obstacle to clarity.

In the last chapter, we looked at what you need to stop believing in order to move ahead. In this chapter, we're going to take a step further and delve into how your attachments are keeping you stuck in place, unable to pivot, and how you can begin the process of releasing yourself from them.

For your pivot, there are two kinds of attachments you need to let go of in order to find increased clarity and move ahead.

The first is an *attachment to the past*. Like I did with my Willie Mays card, you'll discover why we live in the emotions of the past, why they cloud our vision, and how to let go of past hurts.

The second is an *attachment to the future*. Just as you need to let go of your past hurts in order to pivot, you also need to let go of your need for absolute certainty in the form of a step-by-step plan for the weeks and months ahead.

The question for this chapter is: *What are you clinging to that's preventing you from seeing your potential clearly?*

That's what we're about to find out.

1. The Terrible Power of the Past

In May 1995, Di Riseborough's grandmother was brutally murdered in South Africa. Di was shattered by the news, then even further devastated by the discovery that the killers were her own uncle's stepson and his estranged wife.

The crime marked the beginning of a downward spiral for Di and her family.

"My mother never recovered emotionally from finding her mother-in-law's brutalized body," she wrote. "Three months after his mother's murder, my uncle died mysteriously of unknown causes. Two years after that, my own father passed away, his health ravaged by psychological stress and his inability to cope with the tragedy."

Di found herself sinking lower and lower.

For years, she was consumed by anger and resentment. She lost her job. At the worst moments, she would spend hours plotting elaborate revenge fantasies, even going so far as to buy a gun and take shooting lessons. "My anger consumed me," she wrote on her website. "I wanted the bastard dead."

The True Cost of the Past

Most of us don't have to deal with murder as a part of our life story, but all vivid emotional moments from our past are more than simply memorable. They have an unexpected power.

Reliving the pain of losing my prized baseball cards and the feeling of betrayal gave me power. I could conjure up anger about that moment—or others—at any time. I could feel the rush of emotion flood my body. I could summon it and, in my anger, exact what seemed like retribution, over and over. Feeling bad felt strangely . . . *good*.

How can feeling bad feel good? Beyond the feeling of control we gain from being able to revisit negative emotions at will, those emotions actually feel better than nothing. Faced with the choice of either feeling angry or feeling empty, most of us will choose the negative emotion. Anger. Jealousy. Vengeance. Betrayal. Indignation. They're all emotions that feel better than feeling nothing at all. And that makes them critical obstacles to anyone who wants to pivot.

Why? Because, for many people, nothing defines their prepivot life better than the absence of feeling. The further you move from your purpose, the more devoid of emotion your life becomes. You may feel uninspired. Adrift. Flat. Bored. Empty. Feelings such as joy, gratitude, and love disappear and are replaced with an emotional vacuum. And in life, as in nature, a vacuum is always filled. As a result, your life in the present becomes a void that is filled with emotions drawn from elsewhere.

Faced with a lack of joy in the present, you might, then, focus on hurts from the past. Faced with a lack of inspiration or purpose in the present, you might focus your unused energy on rehashing challenges from the past—how you might have reacted differently. What you'd do if you could go back.

But, of course, you *can't* go back. And beyond what you might learn from the experience, looking back at past pain is a fruitless endeavor. More simply put: It's dumb, and you're wasting your time.

In hindsight, I realize that holding on to my anger at my mother was as foolish as holding on to the Willie Mays card itself. Even today, after all these years, the card is worth less than $100—certainly less than the price I paid for it.

Escaping the Prison of the Past

Of course, for Di Riseborough, the stakes were even higher. Remember, her attachment to the past was so great she actually bought a gun.

As time passed and she struggled to come to terms with the event, she eventually moved to Canada and began to put her life back together and follow the path she had dreamed of as a child. She moved alone, with no means of support, but her life improved steadily. Still, she knew she was limited by the pain of the past.

"I was on the path to fulfill the vision I held for myself since age nine," Di told me. "But before I could fully embrace my new path, I had to free my mind from thoughts of this man. I had to face him."

And so, twelve years after the murder of her grandmother, she returned to South Africa and visited her grandmother's killer in prison.

"I sat before him in a plain room," she recalled, "shaking, listening to him express his remorse and regret. I don't remember exactly what he said, just that the experience was so surreal. I shared some of the other consequences of his actions with him, the ripple effect of his brutal attack, and then finally said the words that would set me free: 'I forgive you.' It was one of the most important moments of my life."

"As I turned to leave, I asked him if I could give him a hug," she tells audiences. "He was hesitant at first, but as I held him in my arms, he began to weep, and this overwhelming feeling of compassion came over me. I had truly forgiven him."

Today, through her work as an Intuitive Life Strategist, Di helps others find the courage to deal with their past and life challenges in order to live in alignment with their true nature. She is living the life she imagined for herself at nine years old. And the man who took her grandmother's life? He, too, was forever changed by her selfless act of forgiveness. After serving his term, he was released and wrote Di a letter, thanking her for setting him on the path to live his own true calling.

Identifying Your Past Attachments

Take a moment to reflect on your life. Have you been wronged? Hurt? Of course. We all have. And, more often than not, those past events have a nasty habit of hanging around in the present and preventing us from reaching our potential. They keep us imprisoned. As Di said of her grandmother's killer, "He might have been incarcerated physically, but I was incarcerated emotionally."

The prison of the past is one you must escape in order to pivot. Our job now is to find out where your attachments to the past lie.

Please complete the following statements in complete sentences. Do your best to find several completions for each statement if possible. Set a timer for ten minutes and use the entire time. If nothing comes up in response to the statement, ask yourself how you would respond if you did feel that emotion.

You are giving yourself a rare opportunity to do some deep-healing work, so play at 100 percent from start to finish. Allow yourself to find buried memories, and feel the emotions as they come to the surface. If you start to cry, that is a good sign of release and just means that your body is expelling that toxic energy from your body.

Complete the following statements, reflecting back on the past. You might consider specific emotional events or general feelings about your path in life so far.

1. I feel angry that . . .
2. I feel afraid that . . .
3. I feel sorry that . . .
4. I feel sad that . . .
5. I feel guilty that . . .
6. I feel ashamed or embarrassed about . . .
7. I feel frustrated that . . .

Here are some examples to help get you started:

"I feel angry at myself for staying in a job I can't stand for the last twenty years, and now I feel stuck."
"I feel angry at my parents for not encouraging me to follow my dreams."
"I feel angry at my former company for letting me go after I gave them so many years of my life."
"I feel sorry that I chose safety and security and didn't follow my heart in deciding what to do with my life."
"I feel sad that I let so much time pass without finding my true passion and purpose."
"I feel angry at my spouse for a betrayal."

"I feel embarrassed that I haven't done anything really notable
    in my life so far."
"I feel ashamed that I still have to ask my parents for financial
    support."
"I feel frustrated that I haven't been able to move up the
    ladder in my job."

Choosing to Let Go

Now that you have dug up some of the feelings and emotions that
are part of who you've become, it's time to decide whether you wish
to hold on to those feelings or you wish to let them go.

Is it that simple? You'd be surprised. Letting go may be challenging, but it is most certainly a choice. You can choose to let go, or you
can choose to hang on. Many people choose to hang on to even the
most painful feelings because they think those feelings are serving
them in some way.

For example, "If I let go of this anger it means I'm condoning
what happened" or "If I let go of this guilt it means that I'm a bad
person." Yet we do let go of things all the time. It's likely that in the
past week someone did something to upset you—perhaps they cut
you off on the road or didn't return a call or an e-mail. After some
brooding on your part, did you decide to let the incident go, or did
you determine to hold on to it for the rest of your life? Most of us
let go of the small things but don't realize that the same can be done
with the big things, too.

In *The Untethered Soul*, Michael A. Singer describes the negative energy that we hold on to as "tar" that gets stuck to the most
powerful and vital organ in our bodies, our heart. This negative
energy eventually surrounds and restricts the heart from its most
important function, the ability to emit frequencies and vibrations
of love.

You can make a choice right now whether you wish to continue
to labor with the restriction of your heart energy or release and let

go of what no longer serves you in your mission and vision on this planet.

As the psychiatrist and psychotherapist Carl Jung said, "I am not what happened to me. I am what I choose to become."

If you are prepared to leave the baggage where it belongs, in the past, and choose what to become, you'll find an exercise in the 21-Day Pivot Plan to help you do just that.

From the Past to the Future

Our attachment to negative emotions is a barrier to clarity. To pivot, we need to be able to see clearly in front of us—to be able to clearly see the road ahead. An inability to release negative emotions from the past is like trying to drive by using only your rearview mirror. You can't pivot by looking backward.

▶● PIVOT POINT: **You can't pivot by looking backward.**

But an inability to let go of the past isn't the only thing obscuring our vision. We're just as often trapped by our attachment to the future.

What? Isn't the future what pivoting is all about?

Yes. But not in the way you think. It turns out that your preoccupation with the future might be keeping you stuck just as much as your attachment to the past.

2. Future Attachment: The Siren Call of "The Plan"

In 2005, Keith Leon and his wife, Maura Leon, had written their first book, *The Seven Steps to Successful Relationships*. With an endorsement by Dr. John Gray, the famous author of the Mars/Venus series, and their experience as relationship experts, they expected the book to fly off the shelves.

It didn't quite go according to plan.

"At that point," Keith said, "I didn't know how to market my way out of a paper bag. I didn't know my book was my business card, the key to free press, and my ticket to speaking on the big stage instead of small rooms. We just had a book, and we continued to change lives one small room at a time."

Undaunted, though, they embarked on a new project, called One Million Love Notes, that would deliver digital love notes by e-mail on Valentine's Day. Based on their carefully crafted plan, the goal was to sell a million love notes at just one dollar each.

On launch day, they sold 375.

The couple was devastated. Keith's wife took time off from the business, and Keith decided to forge ahead on a new path.

"I told my wife, 'Just give me the best book title I've ever heard, and I'm off and running.' About a minute and a half later she looked at me and said, 'Who Do You Think You Are?'"

Smitten by the idea but unsure exactly what it meant, Keith prayed and meditated about the book's title. "In my meditation," Keith recalled, "I remembered back to a time in my life when I was in my twenties—a time in my life when I was searching for my purpose. And during that time I had always wished that I could sit down with all the greatest minds in the world, and people that I knew were living their purpose in life. And there it was—I had it: *Who Do You Think You Are? Discover the Purpose of Your Life.*"

In that moment, Keith broke through to a new level of clarity. He had a crystal clear vision of the end result: a book based on discussions with some of the most successful, purpose-driven people who had inspired him. A book that would inspire, teach, and help others find their purpose.

There was only one problem: The way his previous ventures had turned out, Keith knew he needed to move ahead differently than he had in the past.

Deliberate by nature, Keith had a very specific way of tackling his work. "Before, I would always have my list of what I thought I should do. I would take the list and go line item by line item with my agenda, and chip away one thing at a time. But all of this met with very little success."

This time, he knew, he would need a new plan. In fact, it would turn out that what Keith really needed was *no* plan.

Letting Go of "The Plan"

Keith's experience is hardly unique. We've all had setbacks and felt the disappointment of things not going according to plan. What was unique about Keith was his realization that perhaps the planning itself was the problem.

"I decided that how I was doing the business wasn't working—and I wanted to do it completely different than I ever had before. I pivoted right there in that moment. Instead of doing what I thought I should do each day, I would sit down, take a few deep breaths, ask one question, and then sit and wait for the answer. I was calling out to someone or something at a higher frequency than my ego or my little mind to lead me, to guide me, and to show me the way. I would not be moved until I got the answer to the question I had asked."

The answers came, delivered as though by direct download. "I was hearing a voice, and it was telling me what to do next. I just asked, waited for the answer, and took action on what I was told to do. I did this each and every day. The results were a complete about-face from any previous project."

Unplanning

One of the most daunting tasks for prospective pivoters is to face the fact that the path to the life they dream of doesn't come with a ready-made plan.

There's no one-size-fits-all blueprint for going from manufacturing manager to musician. There's no college course to tell you exactly how to become an entrepreneur when your entire work history has been as a salaried accountant.

Believe it or not, though, this is a good thing. You'd have a lot more competition if every pivot were laid out in crystal clear, unfailing steps. But pivots don't work that way. They don't come prepackaged and clear as diamonds.

But of course that's exactly how we want it. The idea that we can make a step-by-step, one-foot-after-the-other foolproof plan feels so safe, so easy, so right, that it's almost impossible for some to resist its siren call. We love plans. Workout plans, business plans, diet plans, life plans—the more plans, the better.

But life doesn't work that way.

And therein lies the paradox of clarity. The more we try to bring an assembly-line precision to change, the harder it is to change. The more we try to force our pivot onto an instruction booklet template, the more it eludes us. *We can't have clarity until we're willing to let go of it.*

So how can we resolve the dilemma? Like Keith, we have to let go of our need for certainty.

For Keith, moving forward without a clear and complete new plan was a radically different way to do business. "The path was revealed to me one step at a time, one question at a time, one answer at a time. This was contrary to how I had always done it before, so for me it was a complete act of faith."

But, trusting his instincts and the voice that led him, Keith took the first step: He made a list of eighty people he felt were living their purpose in life. And then he again asked what he should do.

Armed with the answer, he researched contact information for all of them. Then he began to reach out to them, one by one, and tell them about his book.

Before long, he was connecting with people around the world he'd always wanted to meet. From Bob Proctor to Jack Canfield, from Marci Shimoff to John Gray, Keith was, one step at a time and one day at a time, creating his new project—and his new life. One day it might be a legendary author or speaker, another a famous doctor, activist, musician, or movie star.

It wasn't always easy. Keith had been a planner his entire life. "I had to trust that this voice in my head I was listening to would lead me to where I wanted to go. I had to trust that this voice had my back."

And it did.

Keith is now a multiple bestselling author; the co-owner of a successful company, Babypie Publishing; and a book mentor. He helps people write and market the book they've always wanted to. He speaks at live events and on teleseminars, webinars, and radio interviews. Perhaps best of all, he now counts some of the people who inspired him most—the ones he interviewed for his book—as friends and mentors.

The Pivot Staircase

Keith's pivotal moment wasn't his plan to interview dozens of inspirational figures and share their stories. There is no shortage of ideas in the world, and Keith can testify that a great idea alone simply isn't enough. Keith's real breakthrough to clarity was to realize that the way he had been trying to move forward wasn't working. The moment he acknowledged that his focus on step-by-step planning was holding him back was the moment he began to move forward.

Can you do the same? Absolutely. But you have to accept that your pivot is a process, not a plan.

▶• PIVOT POINT: **Your pivot is a process, not a plan.**

Pivoting is a process, and each step in the process creates the next step. Even as I write these words, I don't know exactly what the next paragraphs will be. I have a goal and direction, even an outline based on the courses I have taught to thousands of people, but each word I write creates the next. Those words create sentences, and each sentence helps create the one that follows, then paragraphs, then chapters, and eventually an entire book. Looking at a finished book or other creation, it's easy to think that it was conceived in perfect form and balance.

In reality, I can tell you it's a whole lot messier.

And here's the thing: Pivoting without a crystal clear plan for the entire path is the same. We still go step-by-step, as if we're climbing a set of stairs in the dark. You may not be able to see more than one stair ahead, but that doesn't change anything. You still move ahead one step at a time. When you reach the top and in the light of dawn look back, the entire staircase, every step, is laid out in perfect, logical, connected order.

You just couldn't see it during the climb.

Much of life is the same. Everything looks clear in hindsight, perfectly ordered, logically connected. The evolution of your career to date makes sense looking back, doesn't it? How you ended up here instead of there, with this instead of that—it all makes sense looking back.

But looking ahead? No way.

Go back ten years in time. Could you have predicted the path that brought you to where you are now? You may be where you hoped to be, but did you get there the way you planned? Most often, the answer is no. We reach our goals—and other things we never imagined—through a path as winding and tangled as a ball of string.

It's the same for everyone. It was the same for Keith, it was the same for The Beatles and Gandhi, and it's the same for you. A good life comes with many things. The one thing it doesn't have is an instruction manual.

▶● PIVOT POINT: You don't need a guaranteed step-by-step plan to get where you're going, only a willingness to take the next step.

Rest assured, you can pivot step-by-step. You don't have to take more than one step at a time.

But you must accept that you can't see all the steps from the beginning. At times you may see several steps. But as the stairs wind out of view, you have to trust that the staircase keeps going. Just because you can't see the steps doesn't mean they aren't there.

There's a word for this type of behavior. It's called *faith*.

> ▶● PIVOT POINT: Just because you can't see all the steps doesn't mean they aren't there.

Can you plan? Yes.

Can you follow the plan? Sure.

Can you deviate? Absolutely. In fact, you will almost certainly have to.

You can plan all you want. You can plan and replan. You can set goals, and list steps to get there. You can do all those things and more.

But you must never, ever let a lack of a clear plan keep you from moving forward. Don't be a slave to the need for a plan. Trust in yourself and your pivot.

When we get to the next part of the book, "Momentum," we'll be introducing you to the Big Pivot Question. It's the most crucial question, the one that begins, sustains, and completes your reinvention.

For now, ask yourself: *Do I have faith that one step will reveal another?*

Clarity Through Letting Go

There's an old James Taylor song in which he sings of the secret to a happy life. The trick, Taylor says, is enjoying the passage of time. It's a profound line, for the only way to enjoy the passage of time is to exist in the *now*, free from rehashing the past and worrying about the future. The secret, then—at least if you're a James Taylor fan—is to let go.

Ironically, attachments do keep us in the present, as Taylor proposes, but it's in a way that denies us the joy of actually appreciating it. Anchored by negative emotions from the past, we relive the worst hurts, the most painful moments. Blocked by fears of the future, we worry and fret about *what if* and *how.*

The result is that we're stuck in the *now* physically, but spiritually and emotionally we're anywhere and everywhere else. We're caught in attachment purgatory.

The solution is to let go. *You need to let go to find clarity.*

Even when we intellectually understand the concept of letting go, it's not always easy. Letting go in principle and letting go in practice can be very different things.

Over the years I have trained, coached, and counseled many people through their pivots, and at some point a critical conversation occurs. As we start to dig into their situation, we discover that the next steps for their pivot are clear. There are opportunities for them—in work, in business, in love, in health—that are right in front of them. There are connections, money, new relationships—there's *hope*—staring them right in the face.

But they won't take action.

At that point conversation either stops altogether or drifts into the story of why they're not ready. "It's not time yet because . . ." or "I'm not ready because . . ." It's a story of past troubles and future obstacles. Of regret and anger, fear and uncertainty. It is, fundamentally, a story of the inability to let go.

If you've found yourself saying those same things when faced with the idea of change, it's important to realize that you're telling yourself that story, too. And as long as you continue to tell yourself the story, you can't let go.

But what's really going on here? Why is it so hard to let go? The answer can be a difficult pill to swallow: If you can't let go, it's because you're not done suffering yet.

When you're anchored to the pain of the past, you're anchored to the pain of punishing yourself, not others. After all, they don't feel the pain of your reliving past transgressions. You do. *And you're not done suffering.*

When you're stuck in the present, waiting for the perfect moment, it's not about the perfect plan. It's about continuing to punish yourself by believing you don't deserve something better. That you're not good enough. It's because *you're not done suffering*.

Sure, you hide that suffering under a story: "Once such-and-such happens, then I'll . . ."

The real story is this: *I'm not done punishing myself yet.*

Which is really a way of saying: *I'm not ready to forgive myself yet.*

Our lives don't change when we're anchored to punishing ourselves. That anchoring disconnects us from the river of infinite potential around us. It keeps us separate from the miracles that are everywhere. From God. From the source. To pivot, you need to reconnect. To let go of the suffering. That's how you reconnect to the unlimited resources and potential around you. All the money, connections, opportunities—they're all flowing past you all the time, but you can't dip in until you forgive yourself and forgive others.

But you can't let go if you can't forgive yourself first.

▶● PIVOT POINT: You can't let go if you can't forgive yourself.

The Next Step to Clarity

It's understandable to be attached to the pain of the past, like Di. After all, the pain is real.

And it's easy, like Keith, to be attached to clear plans. After all, we don't want life to be risky—risk is something we're wired to avoid.

But those attachments keep us stuck. We wait endlessly for the perfect time to arrive, with the perfect conditions that match our elaborate plan. But the conditions never appear. The perfect time never arrives.

The time is now, and we create the conditions by moving forward, unsure of the exact path but determined nonetheless. That is the *Pivot* way: to let go of the past, detach from the plan, and simply allow ourselves to move into the current of change and possibility.

Sound exhilarating? I think so.

But also frightening? That, too.

Does letting go free you from fear? No—far from it. Anyone who dares to dream to pivot is going to face some fear—I suspect you're feeling it now. What it does do is clear the windshield enough that you can begin to see fear for what it truly is and bend it to serve and guide your pivot.

That is where the next chapter on the road to clarity begins.

▶•PIVOT POINTS

> You can't pivot by looking backward.

> Your pivot is a process, not a plan.

> You don't need a guaranteed step-by-step plan to get where you're going, only a willingness to take the next step.

> Just because you can't see all the steps doesn't mean they aren't there.

> You can't let go if you can't forgive yourself.

▶•PIVOTAL QUESTIONS

1. What am I clinging to that's preventing me from seeing my potential clearly?

2. Can I accept that my pivot may need to unfold as I progress?

3. Am I hanging on to negative emotions because they fill a void in my life?

4. Am I refusing to let go because I'm trying to punish someone?

5. If a clear, guaranteed path for my pivot existed, would I take the first step?

6. Am I refusing to let go of the past or the future because I'm punishing myself?

3

Face Your Fear

You gain strength, courage, and confidence by every experience in which you really stop to look fear in the face. You must do the thing which you think you cannot do.

—ELEANOR ROOSEVELT

BY 2008, Kristina Paider had, by most definitions, arrived.

After years of hard work, she'd achieved all the things she'd aimed for: a senior leadership position with a sexy hotel real estate company, a six-figure salary, and a professionally decorated condo with a Chicago skyline view that stretched from the Hancock Tower to the Sears Tower. Life was good.

Except it wasn't. Not really.

"I was spending twelve-plus hours a day in a six-by-six-foot cube," said Kristina, "constantly rushing, battling corporate bureaucracy and nine-month winters. I hated it."

Hate is a strong word. But for Kristina, it was true. What good is a skyline view when most of your waking hours are spent in a cubicle? What good is a prestigious position when it means exhausting yourself day after day with no end in sight?

The answer is that there is no good in it. She was right to hate it. Kristina, like millions of others just like her, was dying a slow death.

By 2013, though, Kristina had already begun to pivot. She'd left her leadership job in Chicago and relocated to Los Angeles to pursue her dream of writing, along with new work. But over time she discovered that she'd succeeded only in trading one life for another similar one. "It was like a trial reinvention," she recalled. "I only replicated what I had in Chicago with slightly warmer weather. It was another model where I worked all the time, so it wasn't really working."

Money was getting short, and something needed to change. Making the leap, Kristina sold everything, cashed in her corporate air miles, and set off on a trip around the world.

As Kristina had been trying to reinvent her life, however, she had developed an inexplicable fear of water. "I was cliff diving in 2003," she recalled, "and I emerged from a jump gasping for air. And I was looking around, going, 'What the heck is going on here? Is there some moss that I'm allergic to?' I was looking all over the place, and someone looked at me and said, 'You're describing a panic attack.' And I thought, 'How can I be panicking?'"

How indeed? Kristina had grown up in the mountains, around water. She'd been a self-proclaimed "fish" since the the age of two. It made no sense. Yet there it was. Over time, she'd gone from cliff diver to someone unable to get into any sort of pool or ocean past her knees. She'd developed a fear that wasn't just affecting her life but that she simply could not understand.

Fear and Your Pivot

Everyone feels fear at some point. It's a part of every pivot. To even consider pivoting, let alone actually doing it, we have to talk about fear. Spoken or unspoken, fear is always there. Whether we articulate it in the form of "What will people think?" or "How will I make ends meet?" or whether it hides just below the surface of conversation like a predator waiting for our first misstep, fear is always there.

But even to say that fear is a part of every pivot is to understate its power. It's also—and this is perhaps more important—at the root of every *nonpivot*.

▶● PIVOT POINT: **Fear is at the heart of every nonpivot.**

By nonpivot, I don't mean an unsuccessful pivot. That's a different thing entirely. To attempt to pivot but not make it on the first try means that you faced down at least some fear. But to never try at all? That's 100 percent pure fear-based. Make all the excuses you want— the economy, your kids, your lack of a degree, your lousy boss, the transmission on your car—but don't fool yourself. A pivot that never starts was blocked by one thing, and one thing only: being afraid.

Fear is the elephant in the pivot room. It's the single biggest barrier to change, yet it's the one that people avoid the most and understand the least.

The reason fear plays such a dramatic role in our pivot process isn't that it blocks our actions. You're going to learn how to do just that—act even while feeling fear—in the pages that follow. The reason fear shuts the process down so effectively is that it is a huge obstacle to clarity. It's a roadblock to deciding what we want and how to get it.

It's impossible to know what you want if fear is obscuring your vision of your future. It's impossible to see and choose the next step on your path if your view is clouded by anxiety. It's impossible to reach even a fraction of your potential without dealing with fear.

When you identify and address your fear, you will find clarity. With clarity, you can pivot.

At first glance, Kristina's growing phobia seemed unrelated to her pivot. After all, what could a fear of water have to do with the anxieties of changing careers? As it happened, though, the two were quite closely linked.

Before we go into that, though, we need to look at why fear exists in the first place.

How Fear Works

According to brain researchers, fear is a product of some of the oldest regions of the brain—the instinctual, unconscious parts way down deep inside that evolved earlier than the outer cerebral cortex, which allows us to be rational and (we think) makes us so darn smart.

When we hear a bump in the night, for example, that sound is received and decoded by our "old" brain in the amygdala, sometimes called the guard-dog part of the brain. It makes a split-second decision: *Is this a threat?* The outcome of that decision can then trigger a cascade of neurochemical and physical changes. Beneath the level of your conscious thought—in fact, faster than your conscious thought—the bump in the night activates the fight-or-flight response. Your heart beats faster to pump blood to your muscles, the hair on your body stands up to make you look larger, you begin to sweat and breathe more rapidly.

For our ancestors who developed it, this response let them perceive and respond to threats faster and survive. Survival meant they could live long enough to reproduce and pass their super fear response on to their offspring. We've inherited this highly attuned survival response. Now we have to learn how to adapt it to our present environment.

This is the take-home message of how fear works: It's a response to a perceived threat, it's automatic, and it's wired into us from the evolution of hundreds of thousands of years. All told, it's a pretty sensible explanation, but the important word here is *perceived*. Our fear response is based on our perception of the world.

But what exactly are we perceiving that's so threatening when we think about pivoting? Unless your pivot involves BASE jumping or becoming a Navy SEAL, you're probably not in much mortal danger.

If you're Kristina Paider, a competent and experienced swimmer and lifelong water enthusiast, what's the mortal danger of standing ankle-deep in water?

The answer is that there isn't any. You're not in mortal danger when you pivot, any more than you're in mortal danger when you stand up to speak to an audience, ask someone out on a date, or negotiate with your boss for a raise—all things that are practically guaranteed to evoke at least some fear response.

But what you are in is *emotional* danger. And your emotions and your physical body are inextricably linked.

While our days as roaming, vulnerable hunter-gatherers are behind us, all of the fear machinery is still there. It's still functioning beautifully. It's a fear factory sitting idle, waiting to be put to use. The problem is that this factory can start up faster than you can blink and change the course of your entire life.

With limited physical threats in our lives, our fear machinery is more than ready to be put to use on more subtle, but no less scary, emotional threats. And pivoting is emotionally scary. Here are just a few of the "threats" that fire up our brain chemistry and activate the fear response:

- What if people laugh?
- What if I lose my money?
- What if I fail?
- What will my parents/friends/spouse think?

These fears represent little physical threat, but they do represent significant emotional threat. Simmering on the back burner behind every pivot, they are far less tangible than heights, spiders, or water but, in many ways, far more serious. It's possible to get through life successfully without making friends with a tarantula. But to pivot you have to face your fear of change.

We're all afraid. We all have the same equipment, same evolution. When we hear the noise downstairs in the middle of the night, our hearts all beat faster without our choosing it. But most of the things we fear in pivoting—*I'm not good enough. I might fail. People won't love me*—aren't the burglar downstairs. They're not a sudden jolt of startling, uncontrollable fear. They're something different. But we still perceive them as dangerous.

Why? What's the harm in even thinking about a career change or writing a novel?

The answer is that although there's no real physical harm, there's a perceived emotional one. Our pivot fears are emotional, manufactured fears that we create over time. They are, in essence, fear stories.

Your Fear Story

At the heart of your fears about pivoting is a story. The concerns about money, the worries about what people will think, the clinging to security—they're all just parts of the story.

The story, if you were to write it down, is absurd. It's unlikely, exaggerated, and in many cases almost comical. I've met people who can't pivot because they're worried about where they'll shop if they change their lives. Yet we tell ourselves our story so many times, and in such vivid detail, that we really believe that it's true. It becomes not just a story but a dangerous reality—something to be feared. The story itself, no matter how unrealistic, plays perfectly to our danger-oriented minds. It becomes a foregone conclusion, and we become afraid.

That means that, in order to change how we deal with fear, we have to change the story.

Like "real" stories in books and movies, comedies and dramas, fear stories have common elements: an inciting incident, a hero and a villain, a plot in which they pursue each other, and a climax.

The same applies to your story. Even though you and your life are unique, your fear story shares the same elements as many others. When it comes to pivoting, there are four characteristics common to all fear stories.

Fear Story Part 1: Fear Means Danger

Fear is an evolutionary adaptation. A jolt of fear and its subsequent rush of physiological changes in the body gave our ancestors an extra edge. In other words, it paid to be scared.

But times have changed. Now our personal safety is rarely at risk, yet we still have all the fear wiring. The result is that our fear response is firing in response to things that really aren't that dangerous. For example, although it's one of the single greatest fears in modern life, it's hard to make a case that public speaking is dangerous. Unless you're a high-ranking public official, standing at a microphone is pretty safe stuff. There's no risk at all, yet for many people the thought of even making a wedding toast is scary.

The same is true when you begin to pivot. The thought of changing your work, taking a financial risk, or moving to another country can send your adrenaline levels skyrocketing. Yet you haven't actually done anything—you're just thinking about it.

That's the first lesson: *Just because you're afraid doesn't mean things are dangerous.*

▶● PIVOT POINT: **Being afraid to pivot doesn't mean you're in danger; it just means you're approaching something new.**

But pivoting, by its very nature, is about doing something new with your life. And that means that the fear you feel is a sign that you're on the right track.

▶● PIVOT POINT: **Fear of pivoting is more likely a sign of clarity than of danger.**

The original purpose of fear might have been to save your life. Now its purpose is to change it.

Fear Story Part 2: The Fearless Hero

Every story needs a hero. And when it comes to your fear story, you don't even have to invent one—the world has already done it for you. Fictional books and movies are filled with fearless, undaunted, utterly confident protagonists who always know what to do and feel no qualms about doing it. And in the real world? We paint our heroes with the same brush. The risk-taking entrepreneur with the "fail faster" mantra. Your successful friend who extols the virtues of bravery. They're all playing the part of Fearless Hero.

The problem is that it's all a lie. The Fearless Hero is the unicorn of pivoting—a mythical creature that exists only because we invented it. It's the part of the fear story that says, "People who do brave things aren't afraid. They just don't feel the fear, and that means they can act."

That's nonsense.

What's essential to understand about fear is that *everyone feels it*. With the exception of people with rare conditions or injuries that affect the amygdala, we're all stuck with the same evolutionary inheritance: We get scared sometimes.

Of course, it doesn't seem that way when we're reading stories of great transformation or accomplishment. We tend to think of those people as extremely brave, or perhaps extremely reckless. We attribute their success to an inability to feel fear, when that's not, in fact, the case.

In the dozens of interviews for this book, almost every pivoter mentioned being afraid. They were all anxious at one point, all nervous about what would happen. They were scared, uncertain, and fearful. Just, I suspect, like you.

The idea that people who dare to live their dreams are fearless is nonsense. Everyone is afraid. The difference is that some people pivot anyway.

▶● PIVOT POINT: Everyone is afraid. The difference is that some people pivot anyway.

Fear Story Part 3: The Quest for Bravery

By believing in the Fearless Hero as part of our fear story, we also fall into yet another part of the fear story: the idea that courage might be waiting for us out there like some made-to-order medical treatment. If only we could get the prescription, we'd be brave enough to pivot.

It turns out that courage isn't something that's granted to a lucky few so that they can act bravely. As the Cowardly Lion in *The Wonderful Wizard of Oz* learned, courage is something you find by acting in the face of fear.

In truth, you are far more capable, intelligent, and powerful than you have ever imagined. You truly have no idea what you're capable of until you try. And when you do try, like the Lion, you'll discover that you were brave all along. You just never gave yourself a chance to prove it.

Like waiting for the perfect moment to change your life, waiting for the day when you're not afraid is a part of the fear story. If you're waiting for the day when you feel brave, you've got a long wait ahead. Bravery isn't the feeling you get that allows you to take action. Bravery is what comes after. It's the tiny seed of confidence that grows a little more each time you take action toward your pivot.

Stop waiting to feel brave. There's no such thing as a fear-free pivot. Everyone feels fear at some point. The question is: *Are you willing to deal with it?*

▶● PIVOT POINT: There are no fear-free pivots.

Fear Story Part 4: The Worst Will Happen

Fear stories can be like runaway trains that *always* arrive at a missing bridge. *If I try to start a business,* we tell ourselves, *I'll have to spend my savings. Then I'll go bankrupt. Then I won't be able to pay my bills. Then I'll lose my home. Then I'll have to live on the streets.*

Then I'll probably die.

That's an absurd story. But in one form or another, this is the story we're telling ourselves: that some unlikely and distant worst-case scenario is almost certain to happen.

Fear stories are disproportional. The stories we tell ourselves are unrealistic, and the risks are exaggerated beyond all common sense. The risks in our fear stories become like the action hero who falls a dozen stories, dusts himself off, and then manages to shoot all the bad guys while backflipping onto a motorcycle. There's just no way that's going to happen.

But that's the way it is with fear stories. They're all about exaggerating danger. They're the result of our minds racing down paths of negative possibilities because that's what our minds evolved to do.

But your mind is just as capable of racing down positive paths. Paths of growth, success, and prosperity. A future of hope and possibility. Dreams that, with a little gumption and a lot of elbow grease, might just come true.

▶• PIVOT POINT: **Fear is almost always based on unlikely extremes.**

Rewriting Your Fear Story

On the north coast of the Dominican Republic near Puerto Plata is a place called 27 Waterfalls, where the Río Damajagua winds its way under the rain forest canopy in a series of spectacular cascading falls and sparkling limestone pools. For a fee, tourists can hike to the top and work their way down by sliding and jumping into pools from heights of almost thirty feet.

Not only was the Dominican Republic the first stop on Kristina Paider's reinvention tour, but 27 Waterfalls would turn out to be the perfect place to face her irrational and growing fear. "I'm either going to succumb to cardiac arrest," she decided, "or I'm going to desensitize myself to the water and get back into it. That was my game plan."

Hiking with a group of strangers, Kristina reached the starting point for the descent. From that point, she and her group began to work their way down a series of increasingly tall waterfalls, jumping off the tops of eight or nine into deeper pools of water below.

As they began to go from fall to fall, Kristina began to have panic attacks with each jump. "My group saw that I was having a little problem, because I kept jumping in and then, you know, coming out, and it was just this dramatic thing that I could not control." Despite that, Kristina worked her way through a series of jumps—and panic attacks—until she arrived at the Big One—a nearly thirty-foot plunge from a rock jutting out into space over the water below.

To make the jump required a leap outward, away from the rock face. Kristina's group suggested she go first, but each time she approached the edge, she backed down. Eventually, her entire group jumped, one by one, leaving just Kristina at the top.

After a few more failed attempts, she gave in. "Finally I said, 'I just can't do it.'"

As she turned to walk away, though, her failure settled on her like a blanket. "I took a step away," she recalled, "and there was such a heavy burden of disappointment and defeat that I did not resonate with. I literally pivoted on that foot, and I just sort of looked away and I just said, 'That is not who I am.'"

And she jumped.

When Kristina came to the surface, the first thing she thought was *I'm breathing! I'm alive!*

In that moment, her fear was gone. "It's hard to put into words," she said. "I was in disbelief."

Kristina would go on to make the Dominican Republic her home. Now she lives there most of the year, working as a writer and consultant. She's been featured in publications from the *Wall Street Journal* to *Forbes* and appeared on CNN. She's been endorsed by

CEOs on seven continents. And the only rushing she does now is to beat the tide so she can walk on the beach to her next appointment. She beat her fear, and she pivoted, too.

But were the two things connected? Did facing her fear change her pivot?

"Absolutely," she said. "You have that moment with yourself where you say, you know, even 'This is who I am' or 'This is not who I am.' And with such strength and such resonance. It doesn't *change* who you are, but it *clarifies* who you are—and who you're not."

There's no better example of rewriting a fear story. In that split second of deciding who she was not, Kristina recast herself in her own developing pivot story. In deciding that being afraid was not who she was, she rewrote the story she'd been telling herself, in increasing detail, for years. As she now says, "I'm all in to jump until I can't jump anymore."

Embracing Fear

You may not have a tangible fear like Kristina's. A fear of water, or snakes, or heights. But you undoubtedly have fears, and they are undoubtedly affecting your ability to pivot.

Tim Jones experienced his fair share of fear when he decided to reinvent himself and his architecture business. Tim was particularly worried about money, a fear common to many people making a pivot.

"I knew I had to do something," he said, "but there was so much fear." Rather than hide from the fear, though, Tim, like Kristina, decided to face it down.

Plagued with worries about money, he decided that rather than not think about what might happen, he would, like Kristina, dive headlong into it. Only, in his case, his dive would be mental and emotional.

"I adopted a childlike faith. I said, 'You know, I'm just going to go for it. What's the worst that will happen? You'll fail. Okay, it's not going to kill me. I've failed before. What's the worst that will happen? You'll go bankrupt. Okay, well, Walt Disney was bankrupt. Donald Trump was bankrupt. So what?' And so I would ask myself these questions. And I would walk through it. I would see it until the end."

Tim's gradual exploration of the worst-case scenario was much like Kristina's gradual exploration of higher cliffs and deeper pools. By mentally preparing himself for the worst-case scenario, he began to build a new "muscle"—a muscle that could lift the weight of fear enough for him to take action.

"When I moved into my office here, I couldn't see the rent and the payroll and all of it. I said, 'Tim, just go for it. The worst that will happen is I'm going to have to move back home to my home office, where I was perfectly happy. If that's the worst that's going to happen, hell, I'm going for it!'"

Tim's approach may seem counterintuitive. Why spend even more time dwelling on the things we're afraid of? The difference with his approach is that it was deliberate. Rather than simply allowing your mind to spiral into increasing levels of anxiety as you fret over any number of potential problems, the worst-case scenario approach goes beyond the worry to ask, "Is this worst-case scenario something I can live with?"

For example, a typical pivot financial fear might be, "I can't afford to start a business. I'll go broke."

The worst-case scenario forces us to ask new questions.

What's the most reasonable worst-case scenario?

Starting a business won't kill you. But there may be some real costs.

What are the real costs of a pivot?

What will it *really* cost to start your business? If your pivot fails, what's the real dollar cost? Can you quantify it?

Can I accept that cost?

If you can accept the reasonable worst-case scenario, what's stopping you?

A Process for Facing Fear

Fear never really goes away. I like to tell students that if you're alive you feel fear—it's a normal part of the human experience, and nowhere is it more likely to rear its head than in times of change.

Although we can't eliminate fear, we can develop a practice to act in the face of it. When I first began to speak to large audiences, it was a daunting prospect, and I used the following practice to help:

1. **Take a deep breath.**
2. **Get present with the fear.** Notice it. Acknowledge that it's normal. It doesn't necessarily indicate danger or a threat. It's simply a response to something new.
3. **Become quiet.** Continue to breathe deeply. This is essential. When we're in a state of fear, our body is shifting into a fight-or-flight response, and our breathing shifts. You can help calm the response by breathing deeply.
4. **Ask yourself:** *Am I experiencing excitement or fear?* You might get onto a roller coaster, for example, and feel something like fear. But when you buckle up and go for it, you realize that it's more excitement than fear.
5. **Ask yourself:** *Will I let this stop me? Will I allow this normal feeling to stop me from moving forward and learning?*

The magic of this process is that it turns a largely unconscious process—the fear response—into a conscious choice. When you begin to assess your choices in a conscious way, more often than not you will make leaps and bounds in your ability not to *remove* fear but to act in the face of it.

And every time you do act? You learn. You get feedback. You might be rejected by a love interest. You might fail at a business. You might be rejected by a man, a woman, a publisher, an investor, a prospect. But if you consciously acknowledge what you're facing and acknowledge your own strength, you'll be able to move forward.

I believe you're built from stronger stuff than you realize. After all, you're part of a lineage of people who survived. You're built from the DNA of people who adapted and who acted in the face of fear. You come from a lineage of warriors. All you need to do is take the time to consciously tap into that legacy.

Fail Faster

It may seem counterintuitive to move toward what you fear. But consider that doing just that is the exact process you went through in your young life. Before you were conditioned by school and work experiences to "not fail," you failed almost *constantly*. Think of your first steps. You didn't learn to walk by going to a weekend retreat to meditate on walking. Instead, you got up, fell down, got up, fell down. *You failed over and over and over.* But each time you stood a little longer, took an extra teetering step. With each failure you *learned*.

When you burned your hand on a hot pot, you didn't cower in fear and give up eating. You learned to use a pot holder. You learned, and as a result you went forward.

Facing your fear—*especially* your fear of failure—is critical to pivoting. In fact, it's so critical that, instead of being afraid to fail, your pivot may just require that you fail *as fast as you can*. Every failure means you learn. Every failure means you can stand up again and take a steadier, better, clearer step forward.

The One Fear

Though all pivot fears may seem different—the fear of public speaking is different from the fear of going bankrupt—there's a deeper truth to the fear equation.

At the heart of all of our intangible pivot fears is one fear: *that we won't be good enough*. People who fear change are people who fear themselves and are afraid to own their true power. They fear the unknown because they doubt themselves as being worthy of the challenge. If we take on the challenge of our pivot and fail, we're afraid that we'll have found indelible proof of our own inadequacy.

The reality is quite different. Each pivot step is like the deeper pools and higher heights of 27 Waterfalls. Even if you "fail" on one step and, like Kristina, come sputtering, panic-stricken, to the surface, that step has taught you something. Whether you see it or not, you've taken one more step, just like Kristina or Tim or thousands of others, toward feeling afraid but changing anyway.

That clarity—the fact that what you're really afraid of is simply not being good enough—provides a new lens through which you can view your reinvention. It's not the pivot that's scaring you—it's what pivoting says about you that is.

When Kristina Paider turned on her heel—literally pivoted—and jumped off the waterfall that day in the Dominican Republic to beat her fear, she wasn't being impulsive; she was tapping into a deep, powerful source of clarity and, as a result, pivot energy. It's a source of power that's at work in all our lives, and one that we, like Kristina, can tap not only to overcome fear but to do things we never thought possible.

What spurred Kristina to jump off the waterfall that day was a decision about what kind of person she wasn't. Was she the kind of person who would let fear dictate her life? Was she the kind of person who would live a life that was less than it could be? Was she the kind of person who was afraid she couldn't? The answer, as she stared down from the cliff top that day, was no. And now she has the fear-free beach life of her dreams to prove it.

But it leaves us with another question on the pivot journey: If Kristina wasn't the type of person who was afraid, what kind was she?

The answer to that question is the next stop on the path to clarity.

▶•PIVOT POINTS

> Fear is at the heart of every nonpivot.

> Being afraid to pivot doesn't mean you're in danger; it just means you're approaching something new.

> Fear of pivoting is more likely a sign of clarity than of danger.

> Everyone is afraid. The difference is that some people pivot anyway.

> There are no fear-free pivots.

> Fear is almost always based on unlikely extremes.

▶·PIVOTAL QUESTIONS

1. What is your greatest fear?

2. How have you handled change in the past?

3. What part of the fear story are you most attached to?

4. What action could you take, however small, that might move you forward?

5. What will it mean to you if you don't pivot?

4

Enter the Pivot
Phone Booth

Be yourself; everyone else is already taken.

—OSCAR WILDE

IMAGINE YOU have a friend who's thirty and recently divorced. She's the sole provider for her young daughter.

Now imagine that that friend has decided to pack up her life and move with her young daughter to Los Angeles to pursue her lifelong dream of becoming an actress.

Would you think she was crazy? What if I told you that she had little prior experience, no connections, and very little money? Would you tell her to turn that U-Haul right around and go home? Or would you tell her to keep on driving?

You might have been faced with exactly that dilemma if your friend was Barbara Niven.

Barbara's wake-up call, and the beginning of her reinvention, arrived in her mailbox. At the time, she was the single mother of a two-year-old and living in Portland, Oregon. She was closing in on her thirtieth birthday when she checked the mail and discovered that her ten-year high school reunion was nearing.

High school reunions are so emotionally charged that entire books and movies have been built on them. For many, few things are so daunting as having to face your former classmates and go through the process of measuring up not just to your peers but to your own fears.

It was no less daunting for Barbara as she read the reunion notice. "It asked me to fill out the normal things," she recalled. "Who I'd married, where was I living, do I have any kids, etc. But the last question was 'Have you achieved all you thought you would in your life by now?' That hit me like a ton of bricks that ten years had already gone by and I hadn't even started! I'd been living everyone's dream of me but my own. That day I hooked back into my true dream."

That true and long-dormant dream was to be an actress. But as a nearly broke single mother, the odds seemed stacked against her. "Everyone told me I was crazy," she said, "that it was impossible. But I found a way in."

Barbara's way in tapped into one of the most powerful pivot tools at your disposal, one that you can put to use regardless of your starting point. It's called *identity*, and it's the next stop on the path to pivot clarity.

The Power of Identity

Decades ago, a plastic surgeon, Maxwell Maltz, began to notice some patterns in his patients.

In many cases, the patterns were positive ones. Patients who were disfigured in accidents would have their self-esteem restored after reconstructive surgery. People who had suffered social abuse all their lives because of physical defects seemed to discover a new strength when the defects were changed by surgery.

None of that seemed particularly surprising. Who wouldn't feel more confident after correcting a scar or a disfigurement?

What was more intriguing to Maltz were those who *didn't* change. "Or what about all the others who acquired new faces," he wrote in *Psycho-Cybernetics*, "but went right on wearing the same old personality? How to explain the reaction of people who insist that the surgery has made no difference whatsoever in their appearance? Every plastic surgeon has had this experience and has probably been as baffled by it as I was."

Adding to his confusion was the fact that some people were disfigured but didn't seem to care and even wore their scars with pride. For Maltz, it was proof that there was something more profound at work.

"I became definitively convinced that many of the people who consult a plastic surgeon need more than surgery and that some do not need surgery at all," he wrote.

What Maltz concluded—and what he spent much of the rest of his life studying and teaching—was that the driving force behind what he saw in his patients' reactions to their surgery, and indeed the driving force behind much of our success in life, was *self-image*.

For Maltz, it seemed to matter far less what people looked like and far more what they *thought* they looked like. It was the image they held of themselves, not the image in the mirror, that determined how they felt and, as a result, how they acted.

Maltz had seen in his patients something that psychologists and social scientists also see: that our *identity*—our image of ourselves and how we fit into the world around us—is a critical piece of how we think, feel, and behave. As a result, identity also determines a large part of the outcomes in our lives.

Clark Kent Versus Superman

If you've ever read a comic book or watched a superhero film, you're already familiar with the idea of identity. Superman adopted the identity of mild-mannered, nervous Clark Kent to hide his true self from the world.

People, like superheroes, have identities. We see ourselves as male or female, mothers or fathers, sons or daughters. We identify as white, black, Asian, Latino, African. We feel urban or rural and identify with various cultural, economic, social, and demographic groups. In high school we might have been jocks or geeks or stoners or goths or band campers or any number of other possibilities. The same applies to our family lives and careers. We adopt identities, and we may change them, depending on context.

Those identities aren't just comic book costumes. They serve a critical purpose. They help us orient ourselves in the world, build social ties, and function and thrive when things are new or confusing, which they often are. Superman's Clark Kent identity enabled him to fit in. To have a job. To be part of a community.

When it comes to pivoting, however, identity can provide us with a secret weapon—a superpower of sorts. To understand how, let's go back to Barbara Niven's pivot.

▶● PIVOT POINT: Identity can be a pivot superpower.

Identity as a Pivot Tool

After the reunion wake-up call, Barbara latched onto her acting dream, but, as with many pivots, the first obstacle was figuring out how to begin. Going from broke single mother to Hollywood actress was a challenge. To gain clarity, she assessed what was within range that fit the role of actress.

"I loved the camera and knew I could write," she said, "so I thought: 'TV news reporter.'"

The challenge? She had no college degree and no qualifications. That was when she tapped into the power of identity. Rather than apply for a job, she just started. She literally became a reporter, right then and there.

The first step? She knocked on the door of the news director at the local NBC affiliate and asked, "If I bring you stories, will you give me feedback?" The director liked her moxie and said yes.

Next she went looking for stories. "I then fibbed my way into places to get stories by saying, 'I am an associate producer at KGW, and I need to interview you to see if you can qualify for a story.' Of course everyone said yes because they wanted to be on TV! So I'd do an interview and then race home to type up a sample script, imagining the shots I'd use if I had a cameraman with me."

Next Barbara took the scripts in to be critiqued, which eventually led to her being hired as an intern.

"As an intern," Barbara said, "you get one shot to be in front of the camera and report a story. When my turn came, I told everyone that I was going to sell mine to the network!" Everyone laughed, but she found a "hook" for her story, and it ran nationally.

From there, she pushed further into acting, auditioning, then screen testing, and eventually landing paid acting gigs.

Barbara Niven would spend the next thirty years making her living in acting. Now she calls herself the "hardest-working actress in Hollywood." A veteran of soap operas and Hallmark and Lifetime movies, at the time I write this Barbara is currently starring on the Hallmark television program *Cedar Cove*. Starting with almost nothing, the single mother found a way to her dreams through the power of identity.

Be-Do-Have: The Superhero Formula

Earning a living as an actor is no small feat. It's something many, if not most, people are unable to do, even without the extra challenges of being a thirty-two-year-old single mother.

Those challenges are practical and logistical. They're more than babysitters and grocery bills. They're also mental challenges deeply programmed into our psyches.

Most people are programmed as children to believe the following: You *do* certain things in life in order to *have* certain things to then *be* someone whom others would respect as a result.

For example, you *do* well in school to get a good job to be able to *have* certain things in life (own a home, drive a nice car, and so on) to eventually *be* someone (a respected member of the community). Here's the way that scenario looks:

DO → HAVE → BE

It's a very effective formula—if you want to spend the rest of your life struggling.

The do-have-be formula is what sets most people on the wrong road in life at an early age and why many never find their true purpose. It's a false promise, conditioned into us from a young age by people who don't understand its flaws.

The flaw in the formula isn't the parts, though—it's the sequence. Barbara Niven, like a lucky few, knew intuitively that *doing* was not the first step in the process. Right from the start, she set aside concerns about what she didn't *have*—experience, credentials, money, connections—and focused on *being* the person she wanted to become. She knew that the secret to success lay with the concept of identity.

When we move identity—the "be" in the equation—to the front of the line, we get this:

BE → DO → HAVE

That is the success equation, and to make the equation work we need to focus first on *who it is we want to become.*

Barbara didn't ask the news director, "Can I have a job?" She didn't even apply for a job. She asked, "Can I bring you stories?" She simply thought of herself as a reporter (be) and, in doing so, behaved like one (do). That allowed her to bypass all the normal requirements of a news reporter, such as education, credentials, experience, and connections, and eventually get a job as one.

And when she went out to find those stories? She didn't ask permission to be a reporter. She simply thought of herself as one and acted accordingly. And after that? She simply followed her reporter identity and handed in the stories to the editor. To start her pivot, she adopted a new identity to replace "single mother." It didn't mean she wasn't a single mom anymore; it just meant she chose to "be" something else, too—to have a new identity.

Barbara calls this "acting as if." She acted as if she were the person she intended to be, as if she had already fulfilled her dreams. She didn't wait until she was ready by someone else's standards; she just acted as if she already were. In her mind, she *became* a person who had what she wanted, *did* the things that kind of person might do, and *received* the results. In doing so, she reversed a common pivot challenge of wanting to *have* instead of simply *being*.

The best part? You can do exactly the same thing.

▶● PIVOT POINT: Focus first on who you want to become, not what you want to have.

Finding Your Inner Superhero

Barbara's story raises an important point about identity. Clearly, we can adopt many identities during the course of our lives, and almost everyone does. We become salespeople, flight attendants, caregivers, community leaders. We are givers, takers, and lovers. We are healed and hurting, broken and whole. As Walt Whitman said, "I contain multitudes."

But which identity matters? Which one will help you pivot? If your goal is to find your true purpose and pivot toward that, the answer is that the identity you need to tap into is your true one.

Barbara didn't invent a new identity—she simply uncovered one that was already there. When Clark Kent went into the phone booth to change, he wasn't there to hide but to reveal his truth, the identity that, like Barbara, mattered most to him and to a world in need. And although you don't need to be faster than a speeding bullet (or kick-starting an acting career), you need to uncover your true self and find a way to bring that to the world.

But, you may be thinking, *Barbara Niven already knew her identity. She already had a dream. She knew her true self. How can I find mine?*

Step 1: Uncover Your True Identity

One of the first books I read after my wake-up call in the emergency room was M. Scott Peck's *The Road Less Traveled.* I could not put that book down, which bordered on miraculous because the only reading material I had at the time was the *New York Law Journal* and *Barron's.*

Reading Peck's book scared me; the experience was like self-psychoanalysis. But when I was done, I knew my self-exploration had only just begun. I was hooked on knowing myself better than I had up until that time in my life. I was hooked on growing organically from the inside out.

The film action star Jackie Chan once said, "I never wanted to be the next Bruce Lee. I just wanted to be the first Jackie Chan." And that's where I found myself. I wanted to be the first Adam Markel.

With excitement and trepidation, I began to examine my life. I had been working all the time, and I had achieved financial success; but instead of feeling happy, I often felt angry, uneasy, and restless. I had trouble maintaining relationships. I sabotaged business deals and investments. I judged, resented, lied, took shortcuts. I lost my hair. I struggled every day, wanting "it" to "work."

The problem was that "it" never worked. Nothing changed.

A pear will never become an apple no matter how long you sit in a full lotus position and meditate on it. No matter how hard you work at planting pear trees, they'll never give you apples. And for years I had been planting the wrong thing.

Finally I began to understand that if you see apples hanging on your proverbial tree of life, you know one thing as sure as you know your own name: The roots of that tree are set for apples, period. If instead of apples you want pears, the only way to get that result is to plant new seeds and grow new roots. That is the way it is in nature, not some of the time but all of the time, and since we are also part of nature, it is always true for us as well.

Uncovering your true identity is about discovering who you are at the level of the roots, at the level of cause, at the level of the unseen. This explorative discovery and process is deep work, both literally and figuratively. It's the kind of work and process that is essential for more successful living and is itself a life's endeavor.

I threw myself into the process of self-discovery and discovered that I loved attending inner-growth seminars—which was new for me then. I especially enjoyed the meaningful teaching of the seminar leaders and the building of relationships between the students. Less than a year later I had a huge *aha!* moment—the one-handed clap, as I now call it.

I realized, *I am also a teacher*.

It was true. I taught swimming at camp when I was seventeen. I began my career path teaching English at Junior High School 185 in Queens, New York. And I had been a lawyer educating the court about my clients' cases for more than a decade. What I had loved about law—the ability to defend, empower, and counsel—was all part of being a teacher. As I'd been drawn further into law as a business, I'd lost touch with that.

In hindsight, it was all so obvious. But at the time, the path I needed to take in order to get back to those roots was obscured. It was the work of cleaning my windshield to find clarity that eventually led me to realize that I had strayed from an essential part of my identity.

Knowing who you are is how you start to design and create a life on purpose. It's the opposite of the default, reactive mode of creation in which so many people are stuck. We're all planting seeds of some sort. And we reap what we sow both unconsciously and consciously in our finances and money, career, health, and relationships. By uncovering your identity, you are planting and planning your life with purpose.

▶● PIVOT POINT: **Your true identity is a signpost to your purpose.**

Step 2: Uncover Your Current Identity Limitations

Like Barbara, I was able to find my true purpose and pivot toward it. And, like Barbara, defining my identity was a critical part of that process. I discovered that not only was I completely out of alignment with my true purpose, but my current path was blocking me from moving forward, and it was actually doing damage to both myself and others.

In my prepivot years, I was quite different from how I am now. I was scrappy, competitive, and quick to argue. I wasn't mean-spirited, but I was feisty. Really, though, what I was was *angry.*

It seems obvious now, but only in hindsight: I was angry because I was living the wrong life. I was off-purpose and miserable. At the time, though, it was just who I was—an attorney. I had adopted that identity. After years of schooling and preparation and years of hard work, I'd become a lawyer, not in the sense of being called to the bar but in terms of identity. I hadn't just become a lawyer the day I got my license to practice or finished law school; I'd become a lawyer over years of gradually adopting that identity. I'd gone into the pivot phone booth a teacher and come out a lawyer.

What's worse, as a lawyer I was in the perfect position to deny, justify, or just plain ignore my growing anger. After all, it was a passionate job that came with a lot of fights. Every case had an enemy. There were always opponents to do battle with. We even had a battlefield—the courtroom—where it was acceptable to go to war. I lived a life where it was easy, even encouraged, to exercise (and exorcise) one's anger every day.

If you had asked if I was angry, though, I would have thought you were crazy. It was part of the job, part of the identity of a Manhattan lawyer. Hard-driving, hard-working, fast-talking, take-no-prisoners, take-charge, make-it-happen. It wasn't anger; it was just life.

Yet I was angry, and it was slowly killing me.

I just couldn't see it. And until I did, I couldn't change. My identity as a lawyer was preventing me from seeing deeper and finding my true self.

◆

It's not enough to discover your true self and purpose. You also need to understand what limitations your current identity and self-image are placing on you. I couldn't move ahead being an angry lawyer and a consciousness-raising teacher simultaneously. Could I still be a lawyer? Certainly—and I continued to be for some time as I worked on my pivot. But I couldn't be an angry one. I couldn't move ahead while I was shackled by the anger I'd attached to that identity.

The problem—and the promise—of identity is that the labels we give ourselves and others come with premade restrictions. "Single mothers," we tell ourselves, "are busy and cash-strapped and have to sacrifice their own dreams in order to maintain stability for their children." It would have been easy for Barbara to stick with the prepackaged single-mother identity. It would have felt safe. She could have easily assumed that, given the barriers inherent in that label, she couldn't possibly do what was required to become an actress, therefore she couldn't have any opportunities to act, and therefore she couldn't *be* an actress. By changing the equation, though, she found clarity. By focusing on her identity first—on *being*—Barbara was able to *do* and then eventually *have* all of the things she lacked when she started out: experience, credentials, money, and connections.

What would have happened to her dream if she had waited until she had all of her ducks lined up in a row? Until some distant day when, perhaps, "single mother" was no longer her identity? What would have happened to her life, her future, her daughter's future, if she had focused on having, rather than on being?

What roles do you currently identify with? How are they holding you back?

Do you hold the identity of "single parent" and perhaps feel that change is not possible? Do you hold the identity of "employee" and as a result see yourself as someone who isn't capable of running a business?

Whatever you identify with can work for you or against you. Your job is to know the difference.

▶● PIVOT POINT: Your identity can work for you or against you; it's your job to know the difference.

Step 3: Surrender to Your True Self

A friend, whom I'll call Maya, has been on a spiritual quest since she graduated from college. For years, she searched for what she called "real and true happiness." She attended retreats, read books, took workshops, all while climbing the corporate ladder in male-dominated Silicon Valley. Yet for years she failed to find what she was looking for.

Maya had been doing plenty of inner work in her workshops and at her retreats, but she was still caught in the do-have-be cycle. She'd been doing the work in the hope of becoming a person who would experience real and true happiness, rather than becoming a person who would experience real and true happiness right from the start. She was a seeker—but a skeptical seeker, often looking for proof of results before committing to the practice.

That all changed when she met Mata Amritanandamayi, better known as Amma, the spiritual leader and humanitarian called "the hugging saint."

When Maya went to meet Amma, she went in with a healthy dose of skepticism but an open heart. When she was hugged by Amma, she felt nothing out of the ordinary. But that night, everything changed. "I was getting up to leave when a woman recommended I stay for the morning ceremony," Maya said. "She said, 'The morning ceremony is extraordinary. It is Mother revealing and gracing us with Divine Mother energy.' I was curious, so I found a spot in the room and lay down on my blanket.

"In the morning, the same woman who encouraged me to stay pushed me to the front of the stage to be near Amma for the ceremony. I was so close to her, I could feel her energy. Suddenly, my heart burst open with a flood of joyful tears. I honestly can't describe the feeling with words. It was incredible."

Maya started carrying a picture of Amma around in her wallet. She began to research Amma and her teachings, to study the results gained by her followers. Still working through her experience with her rational mind, it wasn't until she began focusing on her picture of Amma and asking for help that she began to understand that Amma was her connection to spirit.

"I searched my whole life to find a spiritual connection that would bring me real and true happiness," she said. "But it was only when I surrendered to becoming the person I had hoped to be for years and years that I finally let my mind follow my heart's path."

Maya left her job in Silicon Valley and committed herself to her connection with Amma and to helping people deliver their own transformational messages to the world. She laughs now when she thinks back to her corporate "suit" days. "I'm like a monk now. My main focus is spiritual practice, and that carries forward in the work I do with messengers and change agents, helping them build a strong platform from which to share their teaching with the world."

Sometimes pivoting is as simple as giving yourself over to your true identity, your true self. It's as simple, and as fast, as stepping into the pivot phone booth and casting off the identity that's kept you small, unhappy, and afraid to reveal your truth.

Right now, there's a world in need out there. You have something in you that's worth sharing. You might share that through your job or your business. You might share it through your cooking, your caring, or your collection of poetry. But, like Superman, you have to stop hiding who you are to help yourself—and a world in need.

> ▶● PIVOT POINT: Change requires that you surrender to whom you need to become.

Putting Your Identity to Work

When I was studying to become a transformational program trainer, and before I was ever allowed to present material to any students, I bought a very special microphone that cost more than eight hundred dollars. At the time, that was an awful lot of money to invest in something I might never use even once.

The act of buying that piece of equipment, though, was more than an act of faith; it was an act of identity. I was acting as if I already were a successful trainer, and that act alone spoke volumes to the Universe about my true intention and purpose.

Not long after, I began to work with my first students. And before long I was standing in front of thousands, speaking into an expensive microphone, standing in my true identity, and living my purpose.

You might want to change your job. Your income. Your relationships or your health. You might want to change any number of things about your life and the world you live in.

But at the heart of reinvention, underpinning every change you want, is a kernel of truth: If you want to change your life, you have to change yourself.

In order to *have* a different life, you need to *become* something different. Like Barbara Niven, me, or the untold multitude of Clark Kents of the world, you need to uncover the true identity that's been hidden away. You need to change. And that change needs to happen sooner, not later.

When you begin to think and behave like the person you want to be in the life you want to live, you gain enormous clarity, and you set monumental forces to work. You don't get an acting career so that you can finally be an actress. You start thinking and acting like an actress so that you can have the career.

Barbara Niven isn't the only person who's used identity as a tool to pivot. Every successful pivoter I know has, at some point, simply chosen to be what it is he or she wants to be.

You don't become a writer by *having* a book published. You become a writer when you decide to *be* one. That decision leads you to write every day. That daily habit leads to having a writing career.

You don't become an entrepreneur by *having* a multimillion-dollar company. You first decide to *be* an entrepreneur. Then you do the things that entrepreneurs do, from creating products to selling to recruiting and leadership. Then you can have a multimillion-dollar business.

Robert Riopel, a successful entrepreneur and trainer, experienced this many times as he pivoted toward his true purpose.

"Growing up," he said, "I was conditioned that if you work hard and stay loyal to a company, you'll be rewarded." By the time he was twenty-one, though, he'd been laid off three times, and what he'd been taught just didn't seem to be true.

Robert pivoted from there, delivering pizzas, then becoming a Domino's manager, then a franchisee. But although their income rose, he and his wife found their debts climbing even faster. They had nice things but were constantly working and couldn't enjoy them.

As I did, Robert attended a Millionaire Mind Intensive event. Inspired, he and his wife began attending more and more of Harv's events, volunteering their help wherever it was needed. It was there that Robert discovered his passion for teaching and training others.

"I wanted to teach," Robert recalled. "Harv Eker had been saying he was looking for a trainer, but there were all these criteria. So many hours of training in front of so many students."

Robert didn't meet the criteria. But he had passion. And so he did what so many pivoters do: He just started living life as if he were actually a trainer. "If you have passion about something," he said, "you find a way to begin learning, and you see if it's a fit. For two and a half years I volunteered at almost thirty-eight events a year."

Living in their RV, Robert and his wife helped revitalize flagging pizza franchises in various locations and traveled to every MMI event they could.

One day, opportunity finally met preparation. Harv asked Robert to help him out for five minutes onstage—to do some announcements and send the students to bed. After that, he did the same thing the following three weeks in a row. Next, he got his first tiny teaching opportunity at an event—a brief session as an actual trainer onstage. His *being* was turning into *doing*.

In Los Angeles, in June 2004, Robert stood up in front of 1,200 people and became the first person other than Harv Eker to teach the Millionaire Mind Intensive. Over the next four and a half years he would do more than 120 trainings across North America, help to launch the company in Asia, and live the life he had dreamed of.

Ironically, Robert never did meet the supposed prerequisites to become a trainer until after he became one. His years of experience of simply acting as if he were a trainer gave him the knowledge and experience to become one. Harv would eventually tell him, "The reason I put you onstage that first time is because I couldn't ignore you anymore. You were always there, being of service, and you had an amazing presence."

Robert could have tried to attend school to become a certified trainer or start a business to meet the requisite numbers. But neither of those actions would have opened the door that simply showing up did.

"I don't have any preconceived notions about where I need to start," he said. "I will jump in wherever I have to. Being at those events kept me around the energy and the people. It kept me dreaming and moving forward." Like Barbara, Robert learned that, first, you must *be*—so that you can *do* and then *have*.

The question, then, that you need to ask yourself is not "What do I have to do to pivot?" The question is "Who do I have to become?"

▶● PIVOT POINT: Don't ask what you have to *do* to pivot. Ask who you need to *become*.

Tim Jones, the architect who pawned his most prized possessions to reinvent himself, told me this: "Become what you want, even if it feels like you're pretending. Just be who you want to be, and the world will adjust."

It's a profound insight that I think any successful pivoter would support. Take any action that feels in alignment with the dream you have created for yourself. If you believe you will be a successful business owner, go out and do something that someone in that position would do.

But it does raise another question: How do you know what you want? What if, like Barbara Niven, you don't have a long-standing dream waiting to be dusted off? What if all you know is what you don't want?

That's our next step on the journey to pivot clarity.

▶•PIVOT POINTS

> Identity can be a pivot superpower.

> Focus first on who you want to become, not what you want to have.

> Your true identity is a signpost to your purpose.

> Your identity can work for you or against you; it's your job to know the difference.

> Change requires that you surrender to whom you need to become.

> Don't ask what you have to *do* to pivot. Ask who you need to *become*.

▶•PIVOTAL QUESTIONS

1. What are some of your current identities? Are you a mother? Athlete? Diabetic? Businessman? Artist?

2. How might those identities limit you?

3. What are some of your true identities?

4. Who do you need to become to have what you want?

5

Envision Your Future:
Finding Your Life's Purpose

What is it you plan to do with your one wild and precious life?

—MARY OLIVER, AMERICAN POET

AFTER FAILING at his first two businesses, Vishen Lakhiani decided
it was time to get a job.

There was a problem, however: It was April 2001. The tech bub-
ble had burst, thousands of people in Silicon Valley had lost their
jobs, and competition for the few available openings was fierce.

Vishen persisted, sending his resume to every possible employer
he could think of, and finally landed a demanding, commission-only
job selling technology to law firms.

To deal with the stress, Vishen began to study, and eventually
teach, meditation. As he began to see the profound benefits to in-
dividuals and businesses, the seeds of an idea began to emerge. He
began to look more deeply inside himself and decided that what he
really wanted was to build a business teaching people how to med-

itate. In 2003, Vishen and a partner launched Mindvalley, a digital publisher and marketer of self-help content, with, as he likes to say, "$700 and a beat-up Toshiba laptop in Starbucks."

From its humble beginnings, Mindvalley began to gain traction and find success. But for reasons that are still unknown to him, Vishen was put on a watch list. Suddenly, it became impossible for him to travel by air without long interrogation sessions. Going any-where, even domestically, became challenging, and there seemed to be nothing he could do about it.

Put yourself in Vishen's shoes. You've started your dream busi-ness and found some success. Now you discover that, effectively, you can't even do business in the country you *live* in—a country where every one of your hard-won clients resides. It's an entrepreneur's nightmare.

Finally, in 2005, he and his partner moved the company to Kuala Lumpur, Malaysia, where Vishen had been born and raised before attending college in the United States.

Now he faced a new problem. Mindvalley was still in the business of teaching people how to use meditation for higher performance. But they weren't the only ones. Vishen knew that he could compete, but only if he had the best people in the *world* working for him.

But how do you get the best people in the world to work for you when you can't afford them? And even if you *could* afford them, how do you get them to move to Malaysia?

Enter a new vision: Mindvalley, Vishen decided, would become the greatest place in the *world* to work. It would be the most fun, inspiring, nurturing workplace on the planet. They might not have the most money, but he could focus on everything else that was important that wasn't money. He could create a space where people could grow, be happy, find meaning, and create abundance—all within a business.

It was a tall order for a small business in Malaysia. But a decade later, Mindvalley now employs over two hundred people from more than thirty-five countries. The company has made the WorldBlu List of Most Democratic Workplaces for seven consecutive years, and, just as Vishen envisioned, Mindvalley is considered one of the top places in the world to work.

And Vishen's vision continues to evolve. Mindvalley is also quickly becoming an incubator for entrepreneurs and tech start-ups. Thanks to the company's culture of turning employees into entrepreneurs, there's a Mindvalley business launching somewhere in the world every four weeks.

It would be easy to see the lesson in Vishen's story as simply one of persistence. But that would be missing something even more important. Each time Vishen faced an obstacle, he had to do more than just persist; he had to *pivot*. And the key to each pivot was to *create a new vision*. For every detour, Vishen had to imagine a new way to accomplish his mission. First, a vision for what he wanted to do with his life when his first entrepreneurial efforts failed. Then a vision to build a company around that vision. Then a vision to move that company to the other side of the globe. Then a *shared* vision to attract the critical people he needed to build an outstanding team. For every obstacle, he was able to create a new vision to find a way to success.

And next? Vishen's goal is to give away a *billion dollars* to social causes across the planet via the Mindvalley Foundation by the year 2050. Another vision, another pivot.

Vision Matters for Everyone

Don't be fooled—vision isn't just for multinational corporations. Remember the Lifeboat Game that began this book? You're lost at sea with limited supplies, and you need to make a case for why you should be saved and then move on to the even more challenging task of deciding who should *not* be saved.

After votes are tallied, participants are often devastated that, despite their efforts, others in their group did not vote for them to live.

During the debriefing (and a surprise ending), however, perhaps the greatest insight is when they discover that the key deciding factor for whether they were "voted on or off" the lifeboat was the purpose of their lives. It was their vision for their future that determined whether or not they were saved.

It's a profound example of clarity at work. Those with the clearest vision for their lives are almost always the ones who are saved. It's not about eloquence or effort; it's about *purpose*. That, and that alone, explains why some of them stepped aside and gave up their seats and why others, even after trying desperately to be saved, were not selected. The decision is entirely purpose-driven.

◆

You've completed the first part of your pivot journey and gained clarity. You've learned about the deceptive dangers of the myths around change, about the importance of letting go of the pain of the past and your beliefs about the future. You've learned the link between fear and change and how to use identity as a tool to shape your pivot.

But lurking behind all of these is one critical question: *What do you want?*

Well—what *do* you want?

It's a big question, and it encompasses many others. What is your purpose? What do you want your life to be? What do you want to accomplish? What is the mission of your time on this planet?

Answering those questions is essential to your efforts to find clarity.

Of course, there's no one answer. And the answers—and the questions themselves—shift and change over time as our lives do. But in the short term—in the *now* of your pivot—you'll need to start to create a picture of what you want in order to find enough clarity to move ahead.

After all:

- Kristina Paider couldn't have gone from corporate leader to beach-based consultant and writer without deciding what she wanted.
- Barbara Niven couldn't have taken on the identity of an actress and moved ahead without rekindling her Hollywood dream.

- Keith Leon couldn't have become a bestselling author and publisher without his vision for a book that would help others find their purpose.

In fact, no one can pivot without a vision for what he or she wants to pivot *to*. And that includes you.

Welcome to the next stop on the path to clarity: envisioning your future.

▶● PIVOT POINT: You can't fully pivot if you don't know what you want.

Creating Your Pivot Vision

So where do we begin? Like Barbara Niven, you may already know what you want and just need a catalyst for action. Or, like Keith, you may have a great idea but be unsure of how to carry it out. Or, like many pivoters, you may not be certain of anything at all—yet.

Regardless of where you are on the path to clarity, the following steps will bring you closer to what you want. If you're completely lost and drifting, you'll find a growing clarity of purpose and vision as you work through these steps. If you already know what you want, these steps can hone your vision or save you from the false vision of a life you think you want but truly don't.

Step 1: Let Go of *How*—for Now

It seems so easy to read it, doesn't it? *What do you want?* A simple, innocuous question. The kind a toddler might answer fifty times a day with ease.

If you're like most grown-ups, though, answering that question has become a lot more difficult over the years. There are new bills, perhaps a career you want to protect. You have obligations, debts, responsibilities, and fears you did not have as a child:

- How can I make this meeting and arrange the day care pickup?
- How can I pay both the utility bill and the phone bill?
- How can I plan for retirement?
- How can I meet a partner?
- Do I have time to pick up groceries for dinner?

As we grow older, the logistics of life change. We fall into a world that is driven not by the wonder of discovery—the whys and what-ifs of life—but by the hows. Whether small or large, the challenges of *how* run rampant through our lives. And pivoting is no exception.

Remember Keith Leon, who had to let go of his attachment to planning in order to finally pivot and write his bestseller? He struggled with letting go of the plan for how he would tackle his book. Until that point in his life, the most important thing for Keith when it came to making something happen was *how*.

You might be surprised how much you and Keith have in common. Though you may not feel as though you have an attachment to detailed, written, step-by-step plans, all of us are planners by nature. It's part of the human condition—a magnificent gift of our advanced brain that lets us tackle the trickiest of problems by asking *how*. The second you start to pivot, your *how* mechanism kicks into overdrive.

I'd love to start a business, you think. *Wow! Wouldn't that be great!*

You feel a flash of excitement—perhaps the first one you've felt in a long time.

Then, just as quickly, the *how* arrives and begins whispering in your ear.

How will you raise the money? a voice inside you demands. *After all, you can barely pay the bills as it is. How will you find the time? You're not just going to quit your job, are you?*

Within seconds your excitement is gone, the idea is buried, and the first sprouts of an exciting vision for your future are stomped down before they even had a chance to emerge from the ground.

If you look back, you can probably find times when this has happened. How many times have you dreamed of something, only to have reality, in the form of *how*, bring you out of the clouds and back to earth? Perhaps you imagined taking that extended trip to Europe. Or starting your own bakery. Getting your college degree. Did you have dreams like that in the past?

Of course you did. What happened to them? There's a good chance they were killed by *how*.

How will I pay my bills when I start a business?

How can I afford to go back to school?

How can I possibly take control of my health when I'm so out of shape?

These are all valid pivot questions. At some point, you will have to answer ones like these, and many others, if you plan to reinvent yourself.

But you don't have to answer them now.

In fact, you absolutely should not answer them now. Because the fastest way to derail a pivot in its early stages is to start wondering *how*.

▶● PIVOT POINT: The fastest way to derail a pivot in its early stages is to start wondering *how*.

How is a pivot killer. It's a contagious disease that drives the mortality rate for reinvention through the roof, and you're most susceptible to it early in your pivot.

Right now, we're striving for clarity of purpose, not process. We're trying to see the world and our place in it more vividly. We're trying to imagine a future in which we're happy, productive, and prosperous. And right now, *how* has no place in that picture. There's plenty of time for *how* in the pivot ahead.

So what should you do instead? Shift your focus elsewhere.

Step 2: Identify What You Don't Want

One of the first and easiest ways to begin to shape a picture of your future life is to decide what you *don't* want. Even if you feel completely lost about what you want, you'll almost certainly be able to identify what you *don't*. It's an empowering place to begin.

Are you sick of commuting?

Are you tired of being exhausted?

Have you had enough of someone who disrespects you? Or disempowers you?

Are you tired of being broke?

Are you fed up with laundry? Taxes? Cooking?

What don't you want in your life? If you could snap your fingers and take away the things you hate the most, what would they be?

List them out. Write them down on a piece of paper. Be specific. *Now stop dwelling on them.*

One of the biggest mistakes I made over and over again when I was living in a mode of struggle was to focus on what I didn't want. I would say things like "I don't want to be unhappy" or "I don't want to be working all the time." I would complain, "I don't want to commute to the city today" or "I don't want to get old."

The phrases were different—by that time, I'd found a million different ways to describe what I didn't want—but the energy was the same. Everything was a negative statement of what I *didn't* want to be part of my life experience. They were complaints, and the more I complained, the worse I felt. I thought I had a right to complain because my life felt crappy. Now I know that my life felt crappy only because I spent so much time complaining. Sound familiar?

The problem, of course, wasn't that I had a lot to complain about; it was that I didn't understand the universal laws at work each and every time I made one of those pronouncements. I wasn't seeing the unseen.

Every pivot is different. Every pivoter is unique. But there are some things larger than our individual differences, things that connect us. Laws that are as binding and ever-present as gravity. When you understand and work with those laws, great things become possible. When you work against them, every day is a struggle.

Of those laws, there are two that are most relevant to your pivot. The first is the Law of Attention. I was never aware of why I continued to attract the wrong people and situations into my life until a dear friend of mine introduced me to it.

Also known as the Law of Focus, the Law of Attention states that whatever we focus on expands—we create and attract more of what we dwell on. If you focus every day on how thoroughly your life sucks, your conditioned mind will find ways to prove it to you. You'll see life through the filter of "Everything sucks," and trust me: Everything will.

If, on the other hand, you wake up in the morning and say to yourself, *I love my life,* your conditioned mind will, unconsciously or consciously, look for evidence to prove that your life is worth loving.

Wherever you put your focus, your attention, you also place energy—your own and that attracted from other people and experiences. And wherever that energy shows up, results show up, too. The results can be positive or negative; it all depends on what you focus on. If you simply focus on what you want in your life instead of what you don't want, you will get the result you ask for at least 90 percent of the time.

▶● PIVOT POINT: If you focus on what you want in your life instead of what you don't want, you will get it 90 percent of the time.

My experience in training so many people all over the world is that most folks spend most of their time complaining that their situation in life is unfair. They blame others for the condition of their careers, their finances, their relationships, even their health. They justify their struggles by saying that having more really isn't that important to them. Even though it is.

It would be funny if it weren't so terribly sad. The energy that goes into an hour of good old-fashioned complaining over a cup of coffee could easily be used to create plans for the achievement of almost any goal you could imagine.

Let's replace that complaining and negative focus with something else. In 1935, the spiritual leader Emmet Fox published a short pamphlet called *The Seven Day Mental Diet: How to Change Your Life in a Week*. Fox's prescription was to go a full week without holding or expressing a negative thought. If you slipped up, you had to start the seven-day count at the beginning. It's a challenging but highly rewarding practice and one that pays dividends very quickly. You'll find it in the 21-Day Pivot Plan at the end of the book.

The Law of Substitution

Working with this universal law will instantly change your life, because it will keep you focused on what you want rather than what you don't want. The Law of Substitution works by substituting a positive or empowering thought for a negative thought.

People ask me, "How can I stop thinking crappy thoughts? How can I stop being such a negative person?" If you want to change your negative thoughts, don't try to stop them but rather replace them. Simply get used to substituting an empowering thought for a disempowering one. Yes, it really is that simple. It just takes practice.

If you have an issue with your weight, for example, you might find that you frequently think negative thoughts about your body, your health, and your habits. When you start to ask, *Why am I so fat?* you can stop yourself and substitute a positive statement, such as *I am focused on creating health. I am looking for greater wellness in my life.*

The result? You're no longer focused on the negative, and you're transforming your identity in the process. Your new statements begin to become a self-fulfilling prophecy.

You can find an exercise for building the habit of positive and empowered thinking in the 21-Day Pivot Plan at the end of this book.

Step 3: Find Your Deepest Commitments

A good friend of mine, Greg Montana, is a transformational training expert. He calls the things that you are most committed to in life your "heart virtues." As the term suggests, these are the things in life that you are most committed to at your core. They're the things that show up in your attitude, your responses to situations, and your aspirations. They're the things that give you true joy, not just temporary pleasure. Tap into your heart virtues and connect them to your pivot, and you'll have discovered a whole new world.

I began exploring my heart virtues by closing my eyes and imagining a time when I was seriously angry or upset with another person. Almost immediately I flashed back to an incident when our first child was bullied in school when she was only ten. As I revisited that moment in my life, I could feel my pulse quicken. My skin flushed as I reexperienced that anger, almost as if the incident were happening again.

As I examined those feelings of anger and learned to let go of them, I realized that being bullied as a kid had left me strongly independent and untrusting of authority. As an adult, I became a protector. I routinely came to the rescue of other people. I would stop my car on the road if someone was in trouble. I broke up fights and had zero tolerance for bullying when I was a middle school teacher.

Eventually I became a lawyer who primarily represented the "little guy." Indeed, I came to realize that part of what had led me into that profession was a burning desire to defend and empower people, to help them stay strong in their own lives and not take any crap from anyone.

All of those life experiences were clues to what I was truly committed to. I had realized I loved to teach and counsel, but now I knew that my greatest joy in doing it was when I was helping people live their lives without fear. My ideal—my greatest commitment and burning desire—was to empower people to live in their true higher selves and raise the consciousness of the planet.

Your life can be profoundly transformed by your ability to answer the question "What are you committed to?" From the moment I was able to answer that fundamental question, everything became clear for me. I had clarity in spades. Even the dreaded *how*s were irrelevant as long as I was on a mission to empower and raise consciousness.

▶● PIVOT POINT: **Your deepest values are clues to what you want.**

I routinely ask people attending our trainings, "What time is it?" At first they react by looking at a watch or cell phone. At which point I say, "The time is *now*! The time is always *now*!" Likewise, there's no better time than now to ask and answer the life-altering question "What are you committed to?" Not who but *what*? *What ideals and values are you committed to?*

You can find an exercise to explore your deepest beliefs and commitments in the 21-Day Pivot Plan at the end of the book.

Step 4: Access Your "Beginner's Mind"

There is a concept in Zen Buddhism called *shoshin*, which means "beginner's mind." It refers to being open and eager, holding no preconceived notions about something when you begin to learn it.

I'm fascinated by beginner's mind. I think of it as our inner child, our five-year-old self, who, in many ways, knew more about us at our core than we do now as adults.

As children we all knew exactly what we wanted; we had no angst about our purpose or our desires. But somehow our beginner's mind gets away from us. We *unlearn* who we are. We forget. It's a troubling irony of life that unless we're very intentional, we know less and less about ourselves as time goes by. It's why we feel lost, frustrated, and disappointed. It's why we sense that something's wrong but we can't quite identify what it is.

There comes a point, though, when we want to become reac-
quainted with our true selves—often at some painful moment in
our lives—and we long to know our essential nature and our deepest
dreams again. And so we begin to question. To search.

I believe the answers to that search can be found in the child
mind, and a simple blank sheet of paper can be a great access point.

For this exercise, you'll need a sheet of blank paper and something to draw with.

1. **Begin to draw images of your current and future life.** Do
not worry about artistic merit. This is about scribbles and
stick figures. This is a drawing that only you will see. As
you draw, think of the things that matter to you now. What
you're grateful for. Imagine what you might like to be, do,
and have in the future. Draw quickly, without censorship.
Allow yourself to simply sketch roughly and freely without
criticizing yourself or analyzing as you go.

2. **Identify the future images in your drawings.** These are
the missing things in your life. They represent your dreams,
wishes, and goals.

3. **Describe why you want those things.** For each item you've
identified, especially the things related to how you earn
money, write why you want those things.

Why is crucially important. From my experience working with
thousands of pivoters, I know that the reason people don't reach
their goals is not that they don't know *what* they want; they fail because they don't know *why* they want it.

It's the *why* of our desires that is emotional and heart-centered.
It contains enormous power to drive your pivot forward. And *why*
is often about serving others. When you discover a powerful *why*
that's related to serving others, you'll often have found a unique gift
that you want to bring to the world and a key to your true purpose.

A Letter from the Other Side of *How*

Recently, I received a letter from Bonnie Silver, an attendee at a New Peaks Enlightened Warrior Camp some six years earlier.

In the letter, she spoke of the positive experiences she'd had at the camp. She talked about overcoming her fears and breaking through her self-imposed barriers.

She talked about leaving her six-figure corporate job for more meaningful work. And she talked of earning $40,000 a month in passive income from her business—a business that allowed her also to focus on fulfilling work in the nonprofit world.

I receive many letters like these, and I treasure each one—after all, they're manifestations of my ability to help others find their paths and purpose.

This one, though, was different. Bonnie hadn't just written the e-mail and sent it to me. In fact, the letter wasn't even *to* me. She had written it to herself.

Bonnie had written the letter six years earlier, at the end of the Enlightened Warrior Camp. At the time, she had yet to pivot. She was mired in her corporate job. The letter was from her future self. It was to the Bonnie Silver who had yet to reinvent herself, from the one who had already pivoted and left corporate America behind.

And now, years later, Bonnie can't even see corporate America in her rearview mirror. As she said when she forwarded a scan of the letter to me, "I completely leapt into trusting my intuition and it has served me in my new business. I am well on my way to exceeding my former sales income while owning my life and bringing the letter I wrote many years before to fruition."

That's the power of vision. What's more, it's the power of a vision *articulated*. A vision written down. A story of your life, told not to your friends or family but to yourself.

A story that can be true.

What if you wrote a letter from the other side of *how*? What life does your future self lead?

Testing Your Vision: A Powerful *Why*

At age eighteen, two weeks before his high school graduation, Dennis Kolb had his entire life ahead of him. With a 4.0 GPA, he had already toured the college he planned on attending the following fall.

All of his plans drastically changed when he was diagnosed with leukemia.

"At first I didn't realize the severity of the situation," he explained. "I told the doctor to give me a Red Bull and send me back to class." Instead, he faced more than a thousand days of chemotherapy, spinal taps, and bone marrow biopsies.

At times the challenges seemed almost insurmountable. In the first week of his treatment, he had a bad reaction to the chemotherapy and went into shock. He suffered a tear in his esophagus for which there was no repair surgery. Yeast leaked into his bloodstream, creating a systemic fungal infection. The drug to treat the infection caused further damage to his organs.

His chances for survival went from 60 percent down to less than one-tenth of 1 percent.

"At that point, the chaplain entered my room to give me my last rites and told my family to say good-bye. But I didn't accept that answer, and neither did they," Dennis said.

That night, Dennis fought for his life and survived. But his fight was far from over. Over the next eleven years, he would face many more challenges. He would overcome a prognosis of never being able to walk again due to nerve damage. He had to relearn mathematics due to the devastating effects on his memory of prolonged exposure to chemotherapy.

"I was pushed into a life of Medicaid and disability, far below my dreams and aspirations," he said. "I view welfare as temporary assistance, not a permanent comfort zone, so I was determined to reinvent my life and find my silver lining."

Dennis progressed through years of physical therapy until one day he could not only walk again but he was able to support himself and pursue his passions. "I had to rise above my dreams and discover new ones. Step by step, I opened my heart and mind to a new future."

Now in remission, Dennis is a bestselling author and speaker and the founder of the Rise Beyond Dreams International Foundation, benefiting people facing life-threatening diagnoses, their families, and their friends.

Just surviving was an incredible feat, but it wasn't enough. Dennis had a big *why* motivating him to keep moving toward his vision—he not only wanted to survive, he wanted to help others like him to reclaim their dreams or build new ones. His *why* was big enough to carry him through years of painful procedures and emotional stress. It was big enough to tackle any *how*.

Though I hope your pivot will be nowhere near as harrowing as the ordeal Dennis pushed through, there's no doubt that there will be challenging times. Is your vision strong enough to fuel you through the difficult times of doubt?

▶● PIVOT POINT: **You need a big *why* to power you through difficult *hows*.**

The Power of Vision

After I began to reconnect with my true identity as a teacher, I felt incredibly empowered. It was as if someone had lifted a veil from my vision. I suddenly had more clarity.

But although I had more clarity, I was still stuck. What would my identity as a teacher look like if I expressed it in the real world? There were many ways in which I could fulfill the role of teacher; which was the right one for me? I needed more clarity still. I needed a vision for what my life as a teacher might look like.

I was fascinated by the work New Peaks does in leading trans-formational training programs. When I came across the company, it was doing what I wanted to do. And so I started to create a vision for myself as a successful trainer, speaker, and presenter. Using the techniques in the action plan at the end of the book, I began to create visualizations and painted a vision of my life twelve months later. I envisioned myself traveling the world and training thousands of students. I imagined helping huge rooms of people to make dramatic changes in their lives.

The more I cultivated that vision and focused on it, the more things began to change.

Within six months I was an assistant trainer for Peaks. Twelve months later, I was cotraining large events around the United States. Eighteen months later, I was leading trainings for as many as five thousand people at a time in Asia, the United States, Canada, Australia, and Europe. Within a few years I taught and trained almost a hundred thousand people around the world.

I then became aware that the owner of Peaks wanted to retire and sell his long-standing enterprise. Through the years of trainings, I had learned to follow the most important guidance known to exist: the guidance of the heart. My heart told me to do all I could to become part of the new ownership of the company I had grown to love. I immediately created a new vision of myself at the helm of this amazing company that works each day to change lives around the globe.

I held that vision so close that I could almost taste it. It nearly slipped away on several occasions due to others who were also interested in buying the company. But in the end I realized my vision, and my partners and I bought the company and began a new chapter in our lives.

The Final Step to Clarity

Pivoting isn't always easy.

When I wanted to become a transformational trainer after fifteen years of law practice, I spent eighteen months chasing down the dream on my own time and my own dime. I would fly from event to event, warming up the audiences and dancing with them onstage. I had no promises from the company that I would be successful, and sometimes I was told that I might not have what it would take to achieve my dream.

When I asked Harv Eker, the owner of Peaks, if he would mentor me, he looked me dead in the eye and said, "No!" There was no mention of the remotest chance of a future mentoring relationship of any kind.

Yet less than two years later he was doing just that. And by then I was also the CEO.

There were expenses—big, small, expected, and unexpected. There was time spent away from my family. There were people who didn't approve of me and what I was doing. The list of naysayers, detractors, distractions, and other obstacles was seemingly endless. I definitely discovered that pivoting is not always easy.

But, in the end, the vision won out. Not me, but my vision. It was stronger than I was. All I did was allow myself to be pulled as if by gravity toward what I wanted.

That's the power of vision. That's the power of something bigger than you, bigger than any obstacle.

But there was one thing I had to do before the power of my vision would take me where I wanted to go. It's something that every pivoter must do—and you'll have to do it, too.

You'll have to truly *decide*.

▶•PIVOT POINTS

> You can't fully pivot if you don't know what you want.

> The fastest way to derail a pivot in its early stages is to start wondering *how*.

> If you focus on what you want in your life instead of what you don't want, you will get it 90 percent of the time.

> Your deepest values are clues to what you want.

> You need a big *why* to power you through difficult *hows*.

▶•PIVOTAL QUESTIONS

1. What would it be like to push the restart button on your life today? If you could start over today with a fresh, clean slate, what would you do going forward?

2. What work would you do right now if:

    • Money were no object?

    • You could not fail?

    • You would never receive any status, acclaim, or recognition?

6

Big-D Decide

Once you make a decision, the universe conspires to make it happen.

—RALPH WALDO EMERSON

TEAWNA PINARD started her first business, a human resources company, when she was just twenty-five. Within a year, she'd built it to a million dollars in revenues.

That's impressive growth and a pivot in its own right. But things were far from perfect.

"I'd been working like crazy," Teawna said, "putting in eighty hours a week; at the same time, I was battling a crippling eating disorder. When I wasn't working my tail off to grow my business, I was fighting a losing battle in my body and mind."

It was a battle that Teawna kept up just the same. Over the next decade, her business would become a multimillion-dollar enterprise, and Teawna would continue to build her "picture-perfect" life, complete with designer clothes, a beautiful home, a family, and the money to go with it. "The only thing I was missing was the white picket fence," she recalled, "and I had requested a quote for one of those."

But underneath it all, she was overwhelmed and disappointed. She knew she wasn't really living her life, and keeping up the charade was exhausting.

Finally, one morning it all came crashing down. "I woke up. I looked in the mirror. I didn't recognize who was staring back at me. I realized that most of my life I'd done absolutely everything that my parents and society told me was going to make me feel successful, fulfilled, and award me more happiness. I didn't know who the hell I was."

Balled up on the couch in tears, Teawna was filled with hopelessness, yet wracked with guilt for feeling so empty. After all, she had everything, didn't she?

Salvation arrived in the form of her daughter, two-and-a-half-year-old Savana. "As I was sobbing on the couch, she pulled her little white chair up beside the couch and rested her tiny little hand on my arm, and said to me, 'Mommy, it's okay. I will take care of you.'"

Right then, Teawna knew she had to change. "I knew in that moment that I had to redefine success for myself, and I also knew that I had to make a decision. I knew my own child would live her life for other people unless I decided to get clear on what I truly wanted and take action toward it."

Teawna's turning point is what, in pivot terms, I call a Big-D decision. It's a moment of resolve that happens not at the New Year's resolution level of "cross your fingers and hope" but at a deeper level. It's a moment of true commitment.

Have you ever talked to a former smoker about his or her story? Almost every one of them has a similar tale. They tried to quit many times and failed. They might pick a date on the calendar and say, *This is it.* When the fateful date arrives, they smoke their last cigarette. Then days if not hours later, they find themselves walking out of the convenience store with another pack in their hand.

It's a process that, for many people, continues for years. Then, often after many failed attempts, something changes. Sometimes it's a health scare. Or the death of a loved one. It might be the inability to do something simple such as climb the stairs. It could be a sideways glance from a coworker when they light up outside the office. It could be, like Teawna, the gentle touch and words of a child.

But whatever the catalyst, the result is the same. They decide differently. And they change. Just like that.

Is it easy? No. But in that moment, the decision itself is different. Every decision to quit before that time was a little-d decision. It had no weight. No commitment. No stakes. No emotional power. So it was doomed to fail from the beginning.

A Big-D decision is something altogether different. Whether you Big-D decide or little-d decide, the results after that are almost inevitable. When you little-d decide, you're dabbling. When you Big-D decide, you call forces into being that you may not be able to see, explain, or understand, but they are there just the same. And they're the forces you need to pivot.

▶● PIVOT POINT: **A Big-D decision is a moment of commitment that will summon the forces you need to pivot.**

Identifying the Big D

We make decisions every day, perhaps hundreds of them, ranging from whether to hit the snooze button one more time in the morning to whether to read one more chapter of a book or check the phone one more time before bed. Some are small, such as what to eat, and some are larger, such as whether to replace your car. Or your spouse.

Some of those are Big-D decisions, and some aren't. A Big-D decision isn't your everyday run-of-the-mill choice. It's not like picking a sandwich from a deli menu or choosing who's hosting Christmas this year. Big-D decisions are a different beast altogether. That's something Michael Tran, the owner of Peli Peli, a South African fusion restaurant in Houston, discovered.

Overweight, with soaring blood pressure and a sinking spirit, Michael was a heart attack waiting to happen. "I was on the verge of death," he said. "And not just physically but emotionally." When his doctor told him he needed to take medication for the rest of his life, Michael faced a Big-D moment. "That's when I realized that, you know what? I have to do something drastic or I'm gonna die before I get to see my kids grow up." It was a powerful and frightening realization, but within it Michael had also discovered something else: the fuel to reinvent his life.

That drastic change Michael knew he had to make turned out to begin with adopting a vegan diet for almost a year. He lost weight and got his cholesterol in check.

But that was just the beginning. After regaining his base health, he signed up for an Ironman triathlon, an endurance event made up of a 2.4-mile swim, a 112-mile bike ride, and a 26.2-mile marathon in sequence. Since then, he's completed four more Ironman triathlons and is training for a 100-mile endurance run. And that single restaurant is now expanding to multiple locations.

Before, Michael had felt that his happiness was linked purely to his business success. "For some reason, I was not content with life. If we did well at the restaurant, I would feel happy; if we did not do well, I was sad."

But as the pounds came off, so did the unhappiness and the parts of Michael's life that didn't serve him. "I started just shaving off the stuff I don't need in my life. I didn't hang out with the people who didn't serve me, and I really just started living for my own life so that one day I can be a great father and a great husband for my family. My business took off because now I actually have a real reason to be in business."

How to Know When You've Hit the Big D

Michael's story hits the Big-D highlights perfectly.

First of all, the stakes are higher. Choosing a restaurant for lunch is low stakes. Staring down a heart attack in waiting as Michael did is a much bigger deal. You don't have to quit your job or refinance your home to pivot. But Big-D decisions always involve at least some emotional risk. If you don't feel as though you're stretching yourself, you're not making much of a decision.

Second, Big-D decisions are emotionally charged. If you're picking "just because," that's not a Big-D decision. If you're not seriously excited about your choice, it's not Big-D material. Michael's realization that he might not see his children grow up was a powerful emotional moment.

Finally, Big-D decisions have action behind them. As Tony Robbins says, "A real decision is measured by the fact that you've taken a new action. If there's no action, you haven't truly decided." Michael didn't just decide; he took action, and lots of it.

Those three elements define Big-D decisions. A Big-D decision can truly change your life—just as it did for Teawna, Michael, and millions of others.

But how will you know what a Big-D decision is, and how can you make one? One of the surest ways to know when you've made a Big-D decision is when the idea of starting begins to take over.

Almost all prepivot lives share a common thread of being afraid to take the first step. The aspiring writer doesn't sit at the keyboard. The budding artist doesn't paint. The would-be entrepreneur doesn't make the phone call to find out how much the lease is on the storefront. Why? Because of fear. Fear of failure. Fear of losing the dream. Fear of having to step up and stake a claim for what you really want, instead of just thinking about it. Because the first step—even when it's a small one—is huge.

When you take the first step, you open up a world of possibilities, and not all of them are ideal. And that's just too painful for most people. Better to live with the pain you know than the pain you don't, you tell yourself.

But when you Big-D decide, something happens: The pain of *not* taking action becomes greater than the pain of acting.

Suddenly, to go one more day, one more second, without taking some kind of step toward your dream becomes intolerable. Like the smoker who Big-Q quits in an instant, when you Big-D decide, you become someone different. You become someone who can't stand to be where he or she is for one minute longer.

That's when the magic starts to happen: when you take action to springboard from that Big-D decision and bring your pivot to life. As Teawna Pinard put it, "Everything always starts with making a decision, and I was committed from that moment with my daughter that I would do whatever it took. Whether it took me ten years, twenty years, or a year, it didn't matter. I was committed."

That's a Big-D decision.

> ▶● PIVOT POINT: You've reached a true decision when the pain of *not* taking action becomes greater than the pain of acting.

The Big Pivot Question

Big-D decisions pull from every element of clarity. When you stop believing the myths that keep you from changing. When you let go of the past and your attachment to certainty. When you face your fears. When you discover your true self and then create an inspiring vision for your life. When those things converge, you reach a clarity so obvious and a decision point so powerful and undeniable that the only thing to do is to move forward. That's a Big-D decision.

If Big-D decisions are fundamentally about deep commitment and taking action, the question you need to ask is this: *Am I willing to take the next step?*

This is the critical question of all pivots. First, it reveals if you're ready. If the answer is no and you're unwilling to take the first step, you can't even begin. You're stuck.

Second, if the answer is yes, this question begins your pivot.

Finally, it's the question that keeps your pivot going. It's what sustains your pivot when things get tough. It's a question you can ask yourself again and again, as many times as it takes, until you get where you want to be.

It is, in effect, what creates momentum, which is what the second half of *Pivot* is all about.

So ask yourself: *Am I willing to take the next step?*

▶● PIVOT POINT: "Am I willing to take the next step?" is the question that drives all pivots.

From Clarity to Momentum

Four years after her Big-D moment, Teawna Pinard is now a leadership coach and speaker. She helps women maximize their impact in their business and personal lives. She has three beautiful daughters.

What drives her now? As she says, "I believe that there are no two greater pains in life than not knowing why you were here and knowing why you were here but not fulfilling it."

It's a perfect summation of exactly where we are right now, at the nexus of clarity and momentum. At the point of knowing where we want to go and taking action.

Let's Sum Up Part I

The first half of this book is a journey toward clarity—to a clearer view of your life to date and how you want to live it in the future. So far:

- You've learned to recognize the deceptive myths about change and reinvention (Chapter 1).
- You've learned of the importance of letting go of the pain of the past and the need for certainty about the future (Chapter 2).
- You've learned about the great power of facing your fears (Chapter 3).

- You've learned about the enormous hidden power of identity in shaping your pivot (Chapter 4).
- You've learned about the critical importance of shaping a vision for your life (Chapter 5).
- You've learned about the catalytic power of a Big-D decision (Chapter 6).

In a perfect world, you'd work through these six steps to clarity in sequence. Things would become increasingly obvious, exciting, and tangible. You'd reach the Big-D decision, and *bang!*—you'd be off and running.

Of course, we all know that life doesn't work that way, and neither does clarity.

If you don't feel you have clarity about your pivot, it's okay. You just don't have it *yet*. If you've reached this far and still don't feel that you've made a Big-D decision, fear not. It will come.

Gaining clarity isn't a linear process. You can't always just work through the six steps to clarity in sequence. Each step feeds the others, which in turn feed back to the preceding steps. How, for example, can you create a big vision for your life if you're afraid? It's difficult. But the best way to be unafraid might just be to create a big vision. Each element of clarity not only boosts another, it also requires another. Getting to clarity isn't a straight line but an organic, growing, dynamic process.

Sometimes you need more than just self-reflection to find clarity. Sometimes—perhaps most of the time—a perfect vision of your life doesn't arrive fully formed on your doorstep or during a meditation retreat. A never-ending quest for clarity can leave you, like Maya, on a never-ending quest for . . . clarity.

The missing pieces of the clarity puzzle may come from outside you, from doing real things in the real world. They come from what I call *momentum*, and that's what the second half of *Pivot* is all about.

▶• PIVOT POINT: **Clarity will help you decide, but you can't pivot without taking action.**

►•PIVOT POINTS

> A Big-D decision is a moment of commitment that will summon the forces you need to pivot.

> You've reached a true decision when the pain of *not* taking action becomes greater than the pain of acting.

> "Am I willing to take the next step?" is the question that drives all pivots.

> Clarity will help you decide, but you can't pivot without taking action.

▶•PIVOTAL QUESTIONS

1. Is there a next step that you know you need to take but have been avoiding?

2. Are you ready to take the next step?

3. If no, why not?

4. If yes, when?

PART II

MOMENTUM

Creating Your
Pivot Behaviors

The most effective way to do it, is to do it.

—Amelia Earhart

A Bigger Domino:
An Introduction to Momentum

LIKE MOST people, you've probably had a chance to knock over a few dominoes in your time. A standard domino is a little under two inches high, and if you stand up a series of them in a line and give the first one the gentlest of nudges, you can knock over the entire line.

What's remarkable is how that single tiny nudge can topple a long line of dominoes. In fact, the world record is almost 4.5 *million* dominoes. And there are other records—the number of books toppled "domino-style," the most dominoes toppled underwater, the most dominoes toppled in a spiral, even the most *people* toppled domino-style.

What you're seeing when dominoes—and other objects—topple is *momentum*. In physics, momentum is the tendency of a moving object to keep moving. When one falling domino hits another, it transfers some of its momentum to that domino—just enough to knock it over—and then the process repeats itself.

It's a metaphor that lends itself beautifully to pivots and to the second half of this book. Sometimes a gentle nudge, just a tiny action in the right direction, is all you need to get your pivot started. Once you get things moving, you build enough momentum to move along to the next step in the process.

This simple, game-inspired idea—that you can take one action, which leads to another action, and another, and so on—captures the best pivots perfectly.

Almost.

Because although a chain of millions of dominoes falling over because of one small action is pretty damn impressive, it in no way does justice to the true power of what happens when you set things into motion and begin to pivot. To say that it understates it is . . . well, an understatement.

A toppled domino actually has more than enough momentum to knock over another domino. Once nudged, a standard domino can knock over a domino 1½ times its size. And that larger domino? It can knock over another one 1½ times *its* size. And so on. From there, it's easy to see that you can keep tipping bigger and bigger dominoes, but just how big is actually astonishing.

Imagine starting with a tiny domino, just ⅜ of an inch high. Next to it is a domino 1½ times as large. And next to it, one 1½ times as large again. And so on.

With just a breath of air, you could knock over that first tiny domino. It requires only the barest of efforts. That domino would knock over the next domino—which would still be slightly smaller than a standard one.

But things get big very quickly. So big and so quickly, in fact, that the twenty-ninth domino could knock over the Empire State Building.*

That is the power of small actions, and of momentum. Each action can trigger another that has a little more impact than the previous one. Each action can fuel a larger one that can power yet another larger one in turn.

Momentum, in this way, is like compound interest. It grows, slowly at first, but eventually becomes a snowball rolling downhill, growing exponentially greater with each moment.

---

* http://popperfont.net/2013/01/16/physics-of-the-domino-effect-or-how-to-knock-over-the-empire-state-building-using-28-dominos/.

The first part of this book was about clarity. About clearing the windshield of life so you can create a grand vision for your life that inspires you enough to decide, *This is what I want.*

And now?

It's time to go get it.

Welcome to momentum, and to the first steps of the rest of your life.

The Five Principles of Momentum

In the second half of this book, we're going to explore five principles for building momentum in your pivot. As with dominoes, each step builds a growing energy in your pivot. You'll learn more about both your pivot and yourself. You'll become more confident. More inspired. You'll gain more clarity, more certainty.

And you'll begin to take action.

The principles are:

1. **Baby steps.** Breaking your pivot down into small increments that are less daunting and more doable.
2. **Ritual.** Creating the space, routine, and habits that foster successful pivoting.
3. **Pivot people.** Finding, managing, and working with mentors, stakeholders, and peers.
4. **Resilience.** Facing adversity and using setbacks as a way to move forward.
5. **Growth.** Investing in yourself to create the ultimate pivot advantage.

If you don't feel you have a complete vision for your life yet, don't worry. That's fine, and it's normal. You don't need to stay stuck in Part I of this book, waiting for a perfect vision of your life. Clarity doesn't always arrive shrink-wrapped and preassembled like furniture. Sometimes it arrives in parts. It changes, shifts. You pivot once, then again.

Remember that you can't always see the top of a staircase from the bottom step. Sometimes you need to take a step forward to see where you need to go next. Sometimes, in other words, clarity comes from action.

Let's get started.

7

Baby Steps

I long to accomplish a great and noble task; but it is my chief duty and joy to accomplish humble tasks as though they were great and noble.

—HELEN KELLER, AUTHOR AND POLITICAL ACTIVIST

MY FRIEND Marie had a huge, inspiring vision.

Her dream was to save animals that were abused or unwanted or that had owners who were no longer able to care for them. She wanted her rescue to be world-renowned so that people would seek her out when an animal that she could help was in need.

Oh—and her vision was that they would be exotic animals from all over the world.

This dream is akin to wanting to operate an exotic zoo. The costs of the location alone could be staggering, never mind the medical care, food costs, licensing, insurance, and staff overhead. Marie wasn't talking about putting out some extra bowls of kibble for the neighborhood strays. It was a dream on the scale of millions of dollars.

There are a couple of ways to tackle a big vision like this. The first is to go all in. Marie could build all of the enclosures and barns needed to accommodate hundreds of animals. She could staff the facility and buy all the equipment. She could arrange for feed suppliers, waste removal, transportation, and 24/7 monitoring.

That big-leap approach is a common dream for many pivoters, especially entrepreneurs, and one that's reinforced as part of the bet-the-farm belief that's so pervasive in our culture. "Just bet it all," the saying says. "If you build it, they will come."

The problem is that they don't always come. And in Marie's case, if they did come, they would be expensive, high-maintenance, hungry, and often sick or injured animals. Every one that showed up would cost her more money, not less. "Build it and they will come" would have been a recipe for bankruptcy. A big leap was almost certain to land her in big trouble.

So Marie decided to approach her pivot differently. Instead of adopting a bet-the-farm approach, she'd slowly build the farm, step-by-step, piece-by-piece, and animal-by-animal.

She started by choosing to live in a rural area of Southern California where the zoning would permit farm animals and other agricultural uses. There would be no expensive legal battles to fight, and property costs would be lower.

She bought a house and began to work on her plan to attract not hundreds of abused or injured exotic animals but just one or two soon-to-be-homeless animals. As she was putting her feelers out for animals in need, she developed a small "starter" parcel of her homestead. The barn plans would wait, but for now she put up fences and enclosures for a few animals when they arrived. Step-by-step, she built a small-scale facility. It wasn't her full vision, but it matched the loving care she planned to give to the animals that were yet to materialize. It was aligned with Marie and her values.

Within months Marie received a phone call and took in her first unwanted animal, a cross between a zebra and a horse called a "zorse." Before long she had several zorses. Then a "zonky." Next came a camel and miniature donkeys. And more. So many more, in fact, that she needed to build additional enclosures and take on additional help. Soon people from all over the world began to call her for advice on caring for and healing abused exotic animals. Marie's big dream reinvention was coming true one baby step at a time.

Had Marie gone with the "big leap," she would have been broke before the first creature even arrived. Instead, she took the approach of creating and holding a massive vision for her new life, but she didn't leap before she was prepared to do so; she built her vision in baby steps.

Pivoting in Baby Steps

The surest way to sabotage your reinvention plan is to think big and then leap further than you are prepared for. Breaking your pivot down into tiny, bite-sized pieces has a number of advantages:

1. **It's less scary.** Big leaps can be frightening. Though it might seem dashing and courageous in books and movies, betting your whole life on a business venture or a reinvention is daunting, to say the least. Small steps, however, don't have to be scary at all.
2. **It's cheaper.** Pivots often require investment. It could be in the form of money, time, or energy, but there's always something that has to be put in to get something back out. Baby steps tend to be cheaper than an all-out bet.
3. **It's less risky.** When you bet the farm, you're taking a huge risk. Burning the ships means no going back. But one small step? Not such a big deal—there's only so far you can fall.
4. **You will probably make fewer mistakes.** Not only are small steps less risky, but you might make fewer missteps also. Each tiny step toward your dream gives you more clarity. You learn a little and see a little further. And that lets each successive step be just that little bit wiser. That's

something that can make a big difference over the course of many steps.

These aren't minor matters; they are serious benefits. Not only do they make for a better pivot and dramatically increase your odds of success, the advantages stack up into one giant, critical piece of the pivot puzzle that you can't do without: *They enable you to start.*

The danger with the big-leap strategy for pivoting is not that you might fail; it's that you might never start. And that's the biggest pivot pitfall of all. Big leaps are too scary, too complex. They force you into a state of constantly trying to get your ducks in a row instead of, as the marketing guru Seth Godin puts it, "actually doing something with your ducks."

Never starting is the single greatest pivot killer. Taking baby steps is the solution.

▶• PIVOT POINT: Never starting is the single greatest pivot killer. Taking baby steps is the solution.

How to Baby-Step Your Pivot

If we're going to talk about baby-stepping your pivot, the only way forward, naturally, is to baby-step the baby-step process. Here's how you can use baby steps to turn pivoting from an overwhelming giant leap into something manageable.

Step 1: Break Your Dream into Smaller Pieces

Retired Colonel Russ Barnes is all about breaking down the dream. A decorated military officer, speaker, and author, Colonel Barnes is a master navigator with more than three thousand hours in T-37, T-43, B-52G, and B-52H aircraft. In his nearly twenty-eight years in the U.S. Air Force, he developed a system for getting things done, one step at a time. He used his system—"Routine Achieves Results"—to successfully move up the military ranks, earn several degrees, and, with his wife, raise four sons. Now he helps veterans transitioning to civilian careers reinvent themselves, one step at a time.

Colonel Barnes makes a habit of reverse-engineering his goals. From running a half marathon in under two hours to learning to fly bombers to building a business postretirement, he knows firsthand that anything is possible when you make a plan, break it down into manageable steps, and then take daily action toward the goal.

Recently I had the opportunity to hear about how Colonel Barnes achieved his goal of reading the Bible cover to cover in ninety days.

"I had read passages over the years, but I had never read the entire Bible from start to finish," he explained.

Most of us could make the same claim. The King James authorized version of the Bible contains nearly 800,000 words—the equivalent of reading nearly an entire shelf of individual books. And if you've ever tried reading it, you'll know that it's a task that requires focus. A complete reading of the Bible is nothing like binge-watching your favorite reality series.

Colonel Barnes was determined to read it all, but he knew that to do so would require breaking the big leap of the whole Bible into smaller, more manageable steps. "I broke down my goal," he said, "and determined that if I could read forty-five minutes to an hour every day, I would complete my goal in ninety days. So I got up at four in the morning every day to read. It was a simple step, taken routinely every day, that ensured I would reach my goal."

Colonel Barnes applies the same system in his work with veterans. After they have identified their goals, he helps them break them down into manageable steps—baby steps—that can be completed easily on a daily basis.

Although not every pivot is as simple as dividing things by ninety, you can use the same principle. No matter how seemingly large, complex, or overwhelming, *every* pivot can be broken down—divided from larger leaps into smaller steps.

The starting point for the baby-step process is to simply brainstorm the steps—as you see them now—for your pivot. For example, let's say you want to start a small business making custom furniture. Here are a few obvious things that might jump to mind:

- Learn about entrepreneurship.
- Apply for a small-business loan.
- Buy tools.
- Set up the garage.
- Create a website.

Notice anything about these steps? *They're all still big steps.* "Learn about entrepreneurship" is a step that can take your whole life. "Set up the garage" might mean holding a garage sale, insulating the garage, reroofing, upgrading the electrical supply, and who knows what else. It's a huge step, and that means *it's also a huge barrier*.

The steps are also maddeningly vague. What does "Buy tools" mean? Does that mean spending $20 or $20,000? What tools?

And how about "Apply for a small-business loan"? What if you can barely afford your current debt? That one is so scary it's enough to keep you from even making a list, never mind actually doing anything on it.

The key to successful baby-step breakdown is to ensure that (a) you have the smallest possible steps and (b) the steps are specific.

Learn about entrepreneurship? That might mean buying a book on small businesses. Or signing up for a workshop. Or taking an online course. But which book or course or workshop? The real first baby step, then, might really be "Research the top ten best books for first-time small-business owners." It's small, and it really can't get any more specific. As a result, *you can actually do it*. It's a ten-minute task that you can do while enjoying a cup of coffee in your favorite chair. It's not scary. It's not risky, expensive, or vague. It's not even hard.

You can repeat this process for every pivot step you can think of.

Your breakdown can be a long list or a more free-flowing mind map. Once you have all the steps, you can begin to identify which ones you think need to happen first. Why go to the bank for a business loan if you don't know how much money you need for tools? Why look at tools if you don't know how much space you have in the garage? And why do any of it if it's your first time starting a business and you're not sure how the whole idea even works?

Once you begin to break your list of tasks into the smallest possible steps, you'll be amazed at how many things suddenly seem doable.

▶● PIVOT POINT: **Any part of your pivot can be broken down into easier, smaller, safer steps.**

Step 2: Try It On

If you have kids, you might have participated in a bring-your-son/daughter-to-work day. It's as simple as it is entertaining: You bring your child to your workplace and let him or her see exactly what it is that Mom or Dad does in a day.

The idea is a great ego stroke for parents, a learning opportunity for kids, and a bonding activity for families. It's also a remarkably powerful pivot tool, and one that should rise to the very top of your list of baby steps.

"Try it on" is a career-day-for-grown-ups approach to pivoting. The idea is simple: If you have a job, career, business opportunity, or lifestyle that you've wanted to try, then try it by spending time with someone who's already doing it.

It's that easy. Want to start a restaurant? Open an online store? Become a Buddhist? A vegan? A marathoner? Find someone who's done it and talk to him or her. Better yet, join that person if you can. If you want to start an online business, spend an afternoon with someone who's doing it.

The benefits of "trying it on" are enormous:

Fear reduction. Change is daunting. The idea of transitioning from a career you might have had for decades to something you know almost nothing about is intimidating, to say the least, and it raises that pivot killer of never starting. But what if you could get a risk-free taste of what your "pivoted self" might be in for? You can do so by "trying it on." If you want to be in real estate, there's absolutely nothing scary about simply talking to someone who does it.

Real-world insight. Even if you're not scared by the idea of pivoting, the wisdom you can gain from an afternoon spent in the company of an expert is invaluable.

Opportunity. There's a wealth of opportunity in the try-it-on approach. I've known pivoters who have found business partners, job opportunities, internships, mentors, customers, key suppliers, and investors by doing nothing more than showing a respectful, honest interest in learning more about the lives of others. One minute you're having coffee, hoping to learn a little something about becoming a real estate agent, the next minute you've got an offer to join a brokerage.

If you're thinking "But I don't know any vegans/Internet entrepreneurs/real estate agents/etc.," think again. You probably do. Even if you don't, someone you know probably does. You're almost certainly only one degree of separation from someone who's already doing what you have in mind. All you need to do is ask. If you're into social media, put it out there: "I'm looking for a writer willing to share a few minutes with me to talk about their work." The same applies to the offline world—just ask people. Tell five people what it is you're looking for, and you're almost guaranteed to find your way to a try-it-on source.

Don't be fooled by the simplicity of this step. Exposing yourself to a real-life version of what it is you want can be insightful, reassuring, and intoxicatingly exciting.

▶● PIVOT POINT: "Trying it on" is a low-risk way to test-drive your pivot dream.

Step 3: Get One Done

Whether your passion is to own an art gallery, start a school to teach financial literacy, create an alternative healing retreat, open a creative writing workshop, or start a playhouse for aspiring play-wrights, there is one task you can't avoid: You have to start.

Of course, starting might just be the biggest, scariest baby step of all. Starting feels . . . *big*. It feels like commitment. Like jumping. It feels like something you might just never get around to. Yet starting is critical. It's what kick-starts the momentum you so desperately need to pivot. Until you start, you're an object at rest. And we all know what an object at rest tends to do.

To break that inertia, I use a process I call "get one done." It's the act of taking a single, tangible step toward your pivot.

If you want to own your own real estate business, for example, you will need to first obtain your Realtor's license, and you will need to sell your first house. Yes, you can google "how to become a real estate agent" for months, but eventually something real has to happen. If you really want to become a veterinarian, you will need to start by taking one course and then go on from there. No pivot happens without eventually getting one thing done in the field that you are pursuing.

My brother, a successful New York City attorney, is also an avid collector of "street art." He became so passionate about collecting that he decided he wanted to be a curator of the kind of work he loved. Being a full-time attorney with a wife and four small children, it wasn't likely that he could just become a gallery curator overnight. That didn't stop him, though. He found an artist whose work he thought was very special, and he found a vacant street-level space in SoHo and opened what is referred to as a "pop-up gallery" show-casing the artist and his unique pieces.

That's a good example of how you "get one done." My brother could have talked about doing it until he was old and gray and then said, "Ah, it wasn't that important anyway," or, even worse, "Ah, I regret never making it happen!" Instead, he took one significant, tangible step. It wasn't a huge leap, but it was more than enough to create a whole lot of momentum and gain a whole lot of experience.

That step taught my brother that although the the pop-up model was successful, he didn't want to own a physical gallery. Instead, he wanted to help young artists and raise the profile of the street art genres he loved in other ways. Based on the momentum of his one tangible step, he still practices law, but he now also represents artists in Brooklyn and Manhattan, buying and selling the art he loves and brokering deals for others who love it, too.

▶● PIVOT POINT: Taking one tangible step toward your dream can kick-start the momentum to making it come true.

Step 4: Repeat

The three steps to baby-stepping—break it down, try it on, and get one done—aren't rocket science. In fact, they're obvious. A five-year-old can do them. A toddler uses the same steps to learn to walk.

What makes them so important, and worth describing in detail, is that *you can pivot with just these steps*. As long as you keep repeating them, your pivot will continue to move forward, and your momentum will grow.

When in doubt, break it down. If you can't seem to get the next step in your pivot done, it's probably not broken down far enough. Get more granular. Break it down until the step is small enough that you can take it.

When you're stuck, try it on again. If you're not sure what to do next or you feel you've lost your momentum, go through the try-it-on phase again. Find someone who's done it, and get with them.

And just keep getting one done. Eventually one is five, then many, then an entire pivot.

That's it. With just those three steps you can baby-step your way to freedom.

▶● PIVOT POINT: When in doubt, return to baby steps.

Don't Quit Your Day Job

Lisa Lent was born in San Francisco to a Norwegian mother and an American father. She spent every summer in Norway as a child, which gave her a lifelong love of travel. By the age of twenty-nine, she was an international flight attendant living in London. She loved her job and was following her passion for traveling the world.

In 2000, however, when Lisa boarded a plane in London for one of her regular cross-Atlantic runs to Washington, D.C., her love of travel took an unexpected detour: halfway across, she began to experience chest pains.

"We were so conditioned to work as young people and as flight attendants," she said, "that I actually worked through the flight and a twenty-four-hour turnaround in D.C. and then worked back, because I just wanted to go home." When the pains didn't subside, her mother sent her to the hospital.

Lisa soon learned that she had multiple blood clots in her lungs—a life-threatening condition known as pulmonary embolism. Because the condition isn't always marked by obvious symptoms, it can go unnoticed and can be deadly, causing death in half the people it affects.

The experience changed her. "I had this euphoric feeling," she recalled. "I felt like I cheated death and I was given another chance to redirect my life."

But what would that direction be? Lisa told her mother, "I never want this to happen to anyone else."

And a pivot was born.

Lisa's experience launched her on a journey of health discovery. She learned that the body has an innate ability to heal itself if it's given the right support. And she saw that she could make a difference in providing that support.

Even as she kept working as a flight attendant, Lisa came up with the idea for a packet of vitamin and nutrient pills, called Flight Pack, that would support health during air travel. She'd found the perfect intersection of her experience, her passion, and a market need, and she set to work. Unfortunately, the product launched just a week after 9/11.

For many people, the story might have ended there. But for Lisa it didn't. When her first pivot didn't pan out, she still had the security of her day job and the emotional safety to regroup and try again.

And try again she did. She kept working and searching for her pivot, eventually moving to Santa Cruz, where she met her current business partner.

Today, Lisa is the founder and CEO of Vitalah, creators of Oxylent daily multivitamin drinks. The drink is carried in more than 2,500 stores in the United States and another six countries around the world.

Her advice for prospective pivoters? "I wouldn't quit your day job," she said. "Work very hard to make sure you have an income so you don't have the financial burden or stress."

◆

The opposite of baby steps is a giant leap. It's the huge investment of everything you've got into the dream business. It's quitting your job and heading out the door on a wing and a prayer with no means of supporting yourself. It's "burning the ships," in other words—and that's a myth we dispelled back in Chapter 1.

Lisa Lent's story isn't just one of baby-stepping her way to success. It's also a lesson in the value of actively avoiding big leaps. Of never burning a ship. It was so important to Lisa to baby-step that she kept working during her pivot. The flexibility of her work, and her ability to take voluntary furlough time without quitting, gave her the perfect "no-leap" environment. In fact, it would be more than five years after she founded her company before she officially left her job with United Airlines. That safety net helped her build huge momentum in her pivot—last year, her own company grew more than 50 percent to $2 million in revenue—without the stress of burning her ships.

So what about the people who do make big leaps and find success? That's a gamble that only you can choose. But know this: The stories of big leaps are also the stories that tend to be told. They're sexy and dramatic, and they speak to the part of us that wants overnight success. They speak to the part of us that wants recognition. They speak to *ego*.

Baby steps, in contrast, aren't sexy. But then again, neither is losing your home on a big leap.

And baby steps work. They allow you to pivot with less emotional and financial risk. They help you learn along the way, with fewer mistakes. They help you find mentors, partners, customers, and investors.

But more than anything, they help you start.

And starting is one thing you can't pivot without.

Take Joe Gebbia, for example, whom my wife and I had a social dinner with in San Francisco in about 2011. I had met Joe previously at one of our programs called Mind of Steel, Heart of Gold, and over dinner he shared his story.

A few years earlier, Joe and his roommate, Brian Chesky, were living in San Francisco. Money was tight, and the cost of living was high—they were, in essence, young and broke. The two were struggling to pay the rent. Both had entrepreneurial aspirations but weren't sure exactly what they wanted to do.

When a design conference in the city tied up most of the hotel rooms, the duo got the bright idea to put air mattresses on the floor of their loft and rent them out, breakfast included. They built a simple website to spread the word and got their first customers—three people who each paid $80.

Right then and there, a business idea was born. Why couldn't other people share their homes with strangers and get paid for the experience? And why couldn't Joe and Brian connect those people?

Excited, they forged ahead. They recruited an engineer and a former roommate, Nathan Blecharczyk, to help create an improved website and began to launch their business to coincide with the Democratic National Convention, when hotel rooms would again be scarce. Strapped for cash, they repackaged and sold "Obama O's" and "Cap'n McCain" cereal to raise money. From there they worked their way toward their first "real" investor financing.

In 2009, they received $600,000 in seed capital, and along the way they gave their company a new name: Airbnb.

As of this writing, Airbnb is valued at some $25 *billion*—more than the Marriott hotel chain. What started as three air mattresses on the floor of an apartment now helps more than half a million people find accommodation in more than 190 countries.

The numbers are staggering, but remember: This all started with the simplest of baby steps. Just three air mattresses on the floor, a simple experiment that Joe Gebbia, our dinner companion, and his partner, Brian Chesky, decided to try, *just to see what happened.*

In doing so, they discovered something we teach our students— that thinking outside the box is important, but you need to do more than think. You need to take action. The instructions for getting "outside the box" are on the outside of the box. To get there, you need to move. To take one tiny step.

That's what Joe did. And look where it took him.

So where will you start? What's the first baby step of your pivot?

Every pivot is different, but you might consider starting with the next principle of momentum: *ritual.*

▶•PIVOT POINTS

> Never starting is the single greatest pivot killer. Taking baby steps is the solution.

> Any part of your pivot can be broken down into easier, smaller, safer steps.

> "Trying it on" is a low-risk way to test-drive your pivot dream.

> Taking one tangible step toward your dream can kick-start the momentum to making it come true.

> When in doubt, return to baby steps.

▶• PIVOTAL QUESTIONS

1. What are the first three baby steps that you can take to pursue your dream reinvention?

2. Have you been fooling yourself by waiting for a big step? A stroke of luck, a lottery win, or some future event?

3. Is the fear of a big leap keeping you from taking the first steps to pivoting?

8

Ritual

You should sit in meditation for twenty minutes every day—unless you're too busy. Then you should sit for an hour.

—ZEN PROVERB

WHEN THE economy began collapsing in 2008, Kevin Ward owned a real estate company. After a key partner pulled out, he knew things had to change. He sold the company, merging it with another franchise in Dallas–Fort Worth, where he was living at the time. It was time to pivot.

"I wanted to follow my passion: coaching and training real estate agents," he said. "I decided to move to California."

His first attempt to pivot, however, was short-lived. "I just didn't have the confidence to get it off the ground and really believe in myself—that I could create a business out of it," he recalled.

With his cash flow trickling to zero, Kevin opted to go back into an employee position as a trainer/recruiter for a real estate company. "I just went into survival mode," he said. "I just had to make enough money to pay the bills." But although working at that job paid the bills, it also wasn't his dream. By 2011, he had had enough. "I made a decision. 'You know what? I'm done surviving.'"

Being fed up was a starting point, but Kevin wasn't sure where to go next. He did know, however, that he'd stopped growing. "I had stopped investing in myself. So I started reading again, for my own personal growth, not my job. And then I signed up for Tony Robbins's UPW [Unleash the Power Within]."

About the same time, Kevin attended our free program, the Millionaire Mind Intensive, and within weeks he had joined our Quantum Leap program.

"I told Julie, who was my girlfriend at the time, 'I'm quitting my job. I'm going to give my notice in December.' I launched my company four months later."

At launch time, however, Kevin was broke and only thirty days away from having no income at all. But he forged ahead. "I offered a monthly group coaching program, and I signed up nine people. So I had a total income of eight hundred dollars—a month!"

Three weeks later, Kevin got his last paycheck at work and kept building his business. But things got worse before they got better. He ran out of money. He had to move out of his apartment. He and Julie broke up.

"I ended up renting an unfurnished bedroom in an apartment from a single mom," he recounted. "I slept on an air mattress for nearly a year, and I built my company."

It wasn't easy. Kevin was so broke that he took his lunch to the New Peaks business training events he was attending because he couldn't afford to eat at the hotel. "I didn't have much of a lifestyle," he said. But he persisted. And it paid off. In 2014, Kevin did another launch. This time, he would make $75,000 in seven days.

Things began to change quickly. Kevin and his girlfriend got back together. They were married and could afford the wedding of their dreams. Kevin makes more money than he ever did before, and he has a lifestyle that allows him to stay balanced and happy.

That's quite a pivot. But there's a gap in Kevin's story. How do you go from earning $800 in a month to $75,000 in a *week*? It's a huge leap. What was Kevin doing during those months in an unfurnished rented bedroom that allowed him to pivot so dramatically?

What he was doing, it turns out, wasn't a leap at all. But it was deliberate and persistent. And more than anything, it was consistent. To pivot, he used a principle I call *ritual* to stay focused, stay positive, and continue to move forward, even when things were at their toughest.

The Power of Habit

In *Secrets of the Millionaire Mind*, T. Harv Eker uses a simple metaphor to explain the results we get in life. He argues that your outer world is really a "printout" of your inner world:

> For example, let's suppose you've just written a letter on your computer. You hit the print key and the letter comes out of your printer. You look at your hard copy, and lo and behold, you find a typo. So you take your trusty eraser and rub out the typo. Then you hit print again and out comes the same typo.
>
> What's going on here is that the real problem cannot be changed in the "printout," it can only be changed in the "program."

Harv's simple explanation belies a deep truth: Your reality—the results you get in life—is created by the equivalent of a program (how you think). If you want different results, you need to change the program.

The problem is that much of the time *we're not in control of the program.*

Have you ever been driving and then realized that you have almost no recollection of the last ten minutes? During those ten minutes you made hundreds of minute adjustments to your position on the road. You may have passed other hurtling pieces of steel with only feet to spare. You might have adjusted the volume on your stereo, read a series of billboards, planned your lunch, and thought about an old friend. Perhaps you took a call on your cell phone, drank half a cup of coffee, and made note of the new home under construction on a nearby hill.

For several miles you've been piloting more than two thousand pounds of metal at sixty miles an hour—arguably the most dangerous task you'll do all day unless you're a BASE jumper—and you have no recollection of any of it.

That is the power of habit.

Habits are unconscious neural procedures that we create over time, and they run a huge part our lives without our being aware of them. They're an autopilot of sorts, and in many respects that's a good thing. Without them we'd have a hell of time getting through the day. Remember the first time you drove a car? Imagine if you'd been sent out on the freeway at top speed with a cup of coffee in your hand and told to call the office and resolve a complaint from a challenging customer—without the habit of driving ingrained into your body. You'd have been lucky to arrive alive.

Because your driving skills have been habituated, you can delegate them to the parts of your brain that run automatic programs. That's how you can have amazing ideas in the shower while still managing to wash your hair. It's how you can walk and chew gum or drive and drink coffee. Without habits, we'd be in trouble.

But habits have their downside, too. Smoking is habitual. So is checking your phone when you should be working or focusing on something else.

And habits aren't all physical. We have thinking habits, too. We have automatic mental processes that are triggered just like physical habits. The chime of your phone triggers the habit of looking at the screen without your having to consciously plan to do it. But a setback at work or an argument can trigger a mental habit, too—a state of mind or a pattern of thinking that you fall into without thinking. Mental habits can make us pessimistic and depressed. They can make us angry or lower our confidence. All without our even realizing it.

In fact, our inner world—how we think and feel—is controlled by habits far more than we'd like to believe. Just as we drive on autopilot, we slip into autopilot when we think. Which means that the program Harv Eker talks about that's running most of the time and determining our results is unconscious.

▶● PIVOT POINT: **Your unconscious habits create your reality.**

It all can seem a little dismal at first. Discovering that much of your life is being run by primitive brain wiring without your knowledge or conscious consent can be more than a little disturbing. It's a bit like waking up to discover you've been living in the Matrix.

But learning the truth about habits is also freeing. Habits are, after all, just repeated activities that become automated. You weren't born knowing how to drive; you learned. You drove jerkily at first, weaving across your lane. You learned to back up—awkwardly. You popped the clutch, slammed the brakes, and jammed the gas pedal.

In short, you just practiced until one day you could drink a coffee at sixty miles per hour while singing at the top of your lungs and banging on the steering wheel. Driving might be habitual now, but you built that habit consciously.

So why can't you build other, even better ones? The answer is that you can.

Knowing that much of how you operate is habitual gives you a new tool for change: *creating new, better habits*. To get different results, you need different habits. To pivot, you need to create habits that run the life you want to have, not the life you're already living.

▶● PIVOT POINT: **To pivot, you need to create habits that align with the life you want to have, not the life you already have.**

Pivotal Habits

If you've ever tried to start a new habit, such as exercising or eating better, you have firsthand experience with habits. You also know how difficult it can be—in fact, it can seem downright impossible at times.

Yet forming new habits is critical to pivoting. As Harv points out, you simply cannot get different results until you change the program. And since the program is habitual, *you must change your habits in order to pivot*. You can't start a business, for example, with your old habits. After all:

- Your habit of sleeping in and getting to work just in time won't leave you any extra time to start a business.
- Your habit of thinking *I'm not a businessperson* won't allow you to learn what you need to know to become an entrepreneur.
- Your habit of eating poorly or screen gazing until late at night won't give you the energy you need to invest in your business.

All those things are habits. And for you to pivot, some of them are going to have to change. But how?

The Two Requirements of Habits

At a neurological level, habits are wired connections in the brain that are strengthened over time and with repetition. When you learned to brush your teeth as a child, you did it awkwardly at first, gradually improving until it was effortless and unconscious. During that period, your neural wiring for that activity was being strengthened by repetition. Now your toothbrush habit is so ingrained that when it's triggered—say, by getting ready to leave the house in the morning or getting ready to climb into bed—it happens effortlessly and almost without thinking.

Next time you brush your teeth, try doing it with your other hand. What is normally a mindless task suddenly becomes challenging. Not only will you find it awkward, but you'll discover that your focus narrows to that task alone as your brain tries to process it differently. Whereas you might usually mentally review your to-do list or dream about your upcoming vacation while brushing your teeth, you'll now find you're focused solely on trying to get your hand to move in the direction you want it to. It's a humbling experience.

How can we create new habits? Creating a habit takes two fundamental things: the repetition of the action—thinking or physical—and the actual time to make that happen. You can't, for example, learn to drive well and automatically without actually driving a lot. And you can't drive a lot without putting in time behind the wheel. Spend enough time brushing your teeth with your "wrong" hand, and it will eventually be as easy as with the original hand—but you have to put in the time doing the action.

The same applies to your new pivot habits. You'll need to make time to create them.

But what new habits? Every pivot is different; whether you want to become a landscape painter, a computer programmer, a business owner, or a writer, the job requirements are different. But there are four clusters of habits that are common to almost every pivot.

Education. Personal development is common to every pivot. It's a part of the journey of every pivoter in this book, and it will be part of yours, too. This book is an example. Taking a course to learn how to teach English as a second language is an example.

Good health. You need energy to pivot. Positive energy, and lots of it. Some of that is going to arise out of your ability to develop healthy lifestyle habits. Exercising daily and preparing your own healthful lunch are examples of health habits that can energize your self-reinvention.

Productivity. Pivoting often requires taking on more work. Starting a small business while you continue to work requires you to be more effective. Writing a screenplay while you keep your day job means you'll need to develop a habit of daily writing. The good thing is that you don't necessarily have to do more, you just have to do *better*. Swapping a bad habit (excessive television screen time) for a good one (daily writing) can deliver remarkable results with no extra time.

Mind-set. Your attitude and how you respond to both opportunity and setbacks are critical to pivoting. You need to develop habits that help you foster a positive mind-set, help you understand yourself, and increase your sense of control over your life.

And now the big question: *How do you do it?* Developing habits requires deliberate practice, and that can happen only if you make space for that practice in your life. But if you're like most people, space is one thing you feel you don't have enough of. How can you create the time needed to build the new habits that are desperately important to reinventing yourself? How can you make the time to change your lifestyle and your thinking? To learn new skills? To master a new mind-set around change?

The secret in creating space lies in creating a *ritual*—a master habit for driving momentum in your pivot.

▶● PIVOT POINT: A ritual is the "master habit" for your pivot that allows you to create other habits.

Pivot Rituals

A ritual is simply a sequence of events that's repeated, usually at the same time and in the same place. You can think of a ritual as the "master habit" of your pivot. It's a routine, performed regularly, that lets you build other routines. That's exactly what Kevin Ward was doing in his rented room with the mattress on the floor.

Kevin's ritual is composed of a series of daily practices, ranging from things as simple as drinking water and breathing deeply to exercising, reviewing goals, and journaling. "It's the habits," he maintains, "that really are the foundation, the building blocks, of success. Just having that ritual of doing things is very, very powerful."

Powerful indeed. Kevin's gone from reading very little to reading a book a week, every week. He exercises daily. And his business results speak for themselves.

Remember Keith Leon, who struggled to pivot until he let go of the plan? A ritual was the missing piece—the bridge between over-planning and having no plan at all. "Instead of doing what I thought I should do each day," he said, "I would sit down, take a few deep breaths, ask one question, and then sit and wait for the answer. I was calling out to someone or something at a higher frequency than my ego or my little mind to lead me, to guide me, and to show me the way. I would not be moved until I got the answer to the question I had asked. I started to see flashes, hear the answers, and started to download next steps. I was hearing a voice, and it was telling me what to do next. I would get up and take action on what I was led to do."

Keith's simple ritual helped him go from a failed business launch to a bestselling book and a complete pivot in just one year.

Common Elements of Rituals

Just as every pivot is different, so is each pivoter's ritual. Some people meditate, and others choose simple, quiet contemplation.

Whereas you might begin your ritual with a morning run, another person might begin his or hers with journaling and a cup of tea.

In order for a ritual to work, though, you need to do it consistently. That's why the best rituals have common elements.

Rituals have a morning component. I won't insist that you become an early bird, but consider this: The easiest way to preserve a ritual and protect it from the world around you is to do it first. The morning is the one time of day when you can truly control your time. You may want to place some parts of your ritual in the evening or spread them throughout the day, but if you want to be sure something happens, the best time to do it is when you wake up.

Although Kevin does some things, such as journaling, before bed at night, much of his ritual happens in the morning, before the events of the day can snatch the time away from him.

Rituals are scheduled. The philanthropist Michael Milken is a successful entrepreneur. In the late 1980s, a former teacher of mine was in New York to meet him to discuss a real estate deal. They met in Mr. Milken's conference room. While they talked, someone opened the door. "I hate to interrupt you," the person said, "but this very important deal—they need an answer from you. When can we tell them that you'll have a response?"

Mr. Milken took out his Day-Timer, looked at the calendar, and said, "The next time I have scheduled myself to think is Thursday at ten A.M., so I won't be able to get back to them until Thursday afternoon at five P.M."

My mentor couldn't believe his ears and asked, "Mr. Milken—scheduling time to think? What do you mean?"

Mr. Milken answered, "I schedule time to think. That's what I do. I don't make any important decision unless I've scheduled time to think ahead of that decision."

Mike Milken schedules time to think like he schedules meetings. You can do the same. You don't have to be a billionaire.

Establish a specific time each day when you can think about the most important things in your life. If you're always busy with other things, expecting the right answer to pop into your mind is like waiting for lightning to strike—it's not going to happen when and where you need it to, if at all. Just fifteen minutes, just a few times a week, and you'll find yourself feeling more in control and making better choices than ever.

Rituals are daily. If you exercised for three hours once a month and sat at your desk the rest of the time, would you consider yourself healthy? What if you ate nothing but a salad for a whole day, then fast food for the next twenty-nine? Would you consider that healthy?

For rituals to work, consistency is more important than duration. It's better to do a ritual for ten minutes every day rather than an hour once a month. Why? First of all, habits are built by repetition. Lots of repetition. And doing something twelve times a year is no way to build a habit.

Second, even a few minutes a day is something you can build on. And once you hit your stride, you'll find that time expanding all on its own. One minute of meditation is something you can build on. One push-up a day is something you can build on.

Small and steady builds momentum. Focus on the daily part of the ritual structure and worry less about how long you do something for. You can always make the habit last longer. It's building the habit in the first place that takes time.

Rituals are sacred. Teawna Pinard, who pivoted with a Big-D decision spurred by the help of her young daughter, learned the value of ritual to take control of her time and stay focused on her vision. She also learned the value of keeping her ritual time *sacred* and inviolate.

"There are certain things that are nonnegotiable in my life," she said. "Health is one of them, because I need the energy, the clarity, the focus, to be able to do all the important work that I need to get done. And I need to be able to be present, fully engaged and present, when I'm doing those things. So there are certain rituals that I subscribe to. I used them for years, and they are instrumental in helping me stay on course and laser-focused on my most important tasks and goals."

Teawna's ritual includes meditation, goal reflection, exercise, and gratitude work. And she protects that ritual as if it's a hidden treasure.

Because it is.

Your ritual is the critical space for making your first pivot baby steps. It needs to be carefully protected, nurtured, and grown. It needs to be seen as sacred and treated accordingly.

▶• PIVOT POINT: The best rituals have a morning component. They are scheduled, daily, and sacred.

My Morning Ritual

In the eighteenth century, when he was only twenty years old, the ever-industrious Benjamin Franklin developed a system to improve his character. In his quest for "moral perfection," Franklin committed himself to thirteen virtues. To track his progress, he created a small book of charts, in which he could make a mark each time he violated one of the virtues, such as humility, moderation, or resolution.

Franklin never did manage to achieve his goal of moral perfection, but he did feel as if he were a better and happier man for having tried. And considering he went on to become a successful author, entrepreneur, artist, and founding father of the United States, I would tend to agree.

During my pivot, I adapted Franklin's approach in the form of something I call a Code of Conduct. I have used this Code of Conduct to start my day for more than seven years at this point, and I'm going to share it with you now. My Code consisted of a list of experiences—states of being—that I wanted to experience on any given day. I started with thirteen states just like old Ben. I wrote the states in the form of declarations, such as:

I experience gratitude today.
I experience a positive and harmonious attitude today.
I experience myself adding value to other people's lives today.
I experience a peaceful, easy feeling today.

I experience myself living by a higher standard today.

I experience living in absolute integrity and kindness today.

I experience having faith in my faith today.

I experience myself creating solutions today.

I experience living with a fearless heart today.

I experience myself feeling the presence of God today.

I experience myself being healthy, wealthy, and wise today.

I experience, receive, and manifest miracles today.

I experience forgiveness today.

I still have the original piece of paper I wrote my Code of Conduct on. It's yellowed, faded, torn, and taped, but many years after I created it, I still pick up that worn piece of paper each morning to start my day. It's the keystone of my three-part morning ritual.

1. Code of Conduct

My day starts by sitting up in bed, putting my feet on the floor, taking a healthy pause, and saying, "I love my life." Then I sit in a quiet place for just five or ten minutes. I pull out my Code of Conduct and read through each of the thirteen statements on it. The first one is always gratitude, because it instantly puts me in my heart space. I allow myself to think (and even say out loud) some of the things that I am grateful for—like being alive and breathing, my family, and all the other people sharing the planet with me at this time (things like that).

It takes only a few minutes, but the positive and inspiring thoughts never fail to create a physiological change in me.

2. Eat

I always eat something, slowly. No matter how busy my schedule might be, I take a few minutes to slowly and peacefully consume an appropriate amount of food, remaining in the quiet, meditative state that I created in step 1.

This part of my ritual is indispensible to me. Not only am I setting a clear intention for how I want to live my life, but I can create many of these states, like gratitude and faith, in those first few moments of the day. They're easy wins.

3. Set the Day

Next, while I'm still relaxed and unhurried, I ask myself a critical question: *What is the most important work of the day?* What I'm seeking here is not the most *urgent* task but the most important—the *critical inch*, as Tim Ferriss called it in his book *The 4-Hour Workweek*. It's the most critical aspect of a project, the task that will make the biggest difference to my success that day.

The morning is the perfect time to ask the question. When you focus on the critical inch first each morning, you train yourself to focus on and *do* what's most important, first. And once you've done it? The day is yours. If you want to clean your desk, comb through e-mail, post to social media, or hang out at the water cooler, then go for it. Because if you move that critical inch every day without fail, you'll eventually reach your goal.

I believe that the way you begin your day is the most important part *of* your day. Start right, and your odds of having a happy, productive, intentional day skyrocket. There's nothing superhuman about this morning routine. It costs nothing more than the price of a few bites of food. But the results are miraculous. It takes only a few minutes to create your mind-set, nourish your body, and decide what's truly important, but when you commit to those minutes, you create the foundation for an amazing day.

Building Your Ritual

Now that you understand both the power and the nature of a great ritual, how can you create yours? What are you going to do in your ritual?

Here are a few suggestions that have worked well for many pivots.

Meditate. I tell our students that the mind is like a puppy. If you allow it to do its own thing, it will chew your shoes and eat your furniture. Left to its own devices, it will wreck your house.

Your mind, like your body (and a puppy), needs to be *trained*. And that's exactly what meditation is—it's a discipline for training the mind.

For me, meditation is simply a quieting of the mind in a gentle way. You can allow your mind to do whatever it wants to do without any judgment. Like a puppy, you can gently guide it back to a place of stillness each time it wanders. You can find more meditation instructions in the 21-Day Pivot Plan at the end of the book.

Exercise. There is almost no better way to elevate your mood, boost your energy, and transform your day than exercise. You can move your body any way you choose, but whatever you do, don't be fooled into thinking of exercise as having to join a gym or take a class. A simple walk will deliver enormous benefits. In fact, walking is a habit that meshes with pivoting for many reasons—you get time to think or to connect with others while you exercise. Steve Jobs was famous for conducting meetings while taking a walk. No special skills or equipment required.

Visualize. Many pivoters allocate a portion of their ritual to reconnecting with their vision and their goals by crafting an image in their mind of what it is they want.

Visualization is an amazing practice. All it requires is five minutes of your day. You could make time to visualize after your meditation, gently directing your quieted mind toward visualizing whatever you intend to create that day, in as much vivid detail as possible. For Kevin, it's his goals. He spends seven minutes setting them each day and seven minutes visualizing them.

Write. Journaling is a popular ritual among successful pivoters. The simple act of jotting down the successes of your day, working through emotional events, or capturing the things that strike you as important can be incredibly powerful.

You don't need to be a professional writer to do this. You're not writing for anyone but yourself. You can print in sloppy block capitals with terrible spelling and grammar. Each evening, Kevin lists five things he's grateful for and five "wins" from the day.

Read. Andrew Carnegie called libraries a "never-failing spring in the desert," and books are a never-failing means of support for your pivot. Whether you need help for a specific task, strategies for personal growth, or just a boost of inspiration for your own life change, reading is an essential part of any ritual.

Don't consider yourself a reader? Consider listening to audiobooks instead. You can turn your daily drive or walk into an opportunity to learn.

Review. Kevin Ward's ritual includes reviewing his goals daily. "It was mind-boggling to realize," he said, "how much you're accomplishing when you have clarity. You start seeing it and you go, 'Wow. I get stuff done.'"

Kevin uses a goal-tracking system and moves goals from one list to another after they're completed. After tracking himself this way for some time, Kevin was amazed to discover that he was getting hundreds of things done—more than 160 goals in 2014 alone.

Appreciate. I begin every day the exact same way: I wake up, put my feet on the floor, and say, "I love my life." In doing so, not only am I expressing gratitude—believe me, I truly do love my life—but I'm also placing my attention in a specific place. I'm starting the day with a focus on the positive, not the negative. Gratitude is a well-established strategy for increased happiness—not a bad return for a few moments a day.

Celebrate. Don't be afraid to carve out special times in your ritual to acknowledge how far you've come. It's not just self-congratulation but also a special form of gratitude that acknowledges the results of your efforts. Don't diminish your progress by failing to recognize even a small win.

You don't need to do all these things daily. The great thing about rituals is that they're yours. You get to decide which ones will be your everyday practice and which to add on when appropriate. Just remember that the objective is to build new habits to fuel momentum in your pivot. That means consistency trumps all. Start small—as small as you can—and slowly build. Think *daily* and construct your ritual accordingly.

Habits Take Time to Develop

Remember, you're not going to do this perfectly right away. Right now you're operating on habits that have been with you almost your entire life. So cut yourself some slack.

Start easy. Think you don't have time? Commit to *one minute a day*. Just one minute each morning. It's so small, you can't make an excuse not to do it. And it's so small, it's not scary. It's so small that it's truly sustainable.

One minute of quiet thought, in the same place at the same time, is something you can begin and sustain. A commitment to meditate for twenty minutes, hit the gym, read a book, plan your day, and repeat affirmations is a recipe for early failure.

Don't worry if you miss a day. Don't let one missed day spoil your change. If you miss a day, just pick up again the next day where you left off. Kevin's ritual, at first, happened only about 30 percent of the time. But he continually recommitted, increasing his ritual until he had done some elements almost every day for a year. "By then," he said, "I had it internalized."

Use simple tracking. Get a calendar and mark each day you do your ritual. You'll be surprised at how much you can accomplish and how inspiring an unbroken chain of "ritual days" can be.

▶● PIVOT POINT: To build habits, focus on consistency. Start easy and grow.

Ritual as Momentum

Ritual is the missing link between a step-by-step pivot plan and a complete seat-of-the pants reinvention. It brings the reassuring predictability of routine but allows for flow, creativity, and flexibility. It lets you feel sure while you stay adaptable. It's also such a critical part of your pivot that when you reach the action plan at the end of this book, you'll discover it's one of the very first steps in pivoting.

Rituals are also about creating space—the time, mental clarity, and even physical space to reinvent yourself. Although Kevin's finances were troubled, they forced him to simplify his life, which left him with fewer things to manage and maintain and more time and mental space to focus on his business.

Do you need to sell your home to pivot? No. But it's worth considering how you might bring the idea of simplicity to your world. Can you declutter? Can you reduce or eliminate obligations that are bogging you down? Can you simplify your finances? Balance your budget? Some of the great entrepreneurs and great minds of history, such as Steve Jobs and Albert Einstein, wore the same style of clothes every day to simplify their lives and leave them more time to focus on what was most important to them.

Perhaps one of the great hidden results of ritual, though, is the increased sense of productivity and control. A morning ritual is something that's yours. It's happening at a time that you create and you control. No one can take it from you unless you choose to let them. It's a time for you and your pivot dreams.

Every day that you go through your ritual, you move your pivot forward. You change your program to something that better serves your reinvention. Your identity begins to shift—you become the kind of person who seizes the day, who makes things happen. You relabel yourself. You gain momentum. As Kevin said, "I'm not a procrastinator anymore. I'm a doer."

▶● PIVOT POINT: **Rituals are about creating mental, temporal, and physical space in which to build momentum.**

Of course, Kevin didn't pivot by spending all his time meditating in his office. As the saying goes, you need to "pray, but move your feet."

Kevin used his ritual to build momentum. To take action.

What action? As every successful pivoter knows, change doesn't happen in a vacuum. You can't pivot alone.

You need other people. That's the subject of the next chapter.

▶·PIVOT POINTS

> Your unconscious habits create your reality.

> To pivot, you need to create habits that align with the life you want to have, not the life you already have.

> A ritual is the "master habit" for your pivot that allows you to create other habits.

> The best rituals have a morning component. They are scheduled, daily, and sacred.

> To build habits, focus on consistency. Start easy and grow.

> Rituals are about creating mental, temporal, and physical space in which to build momentum.

▶•PIVOTAL QUESTIONS

1. How can you reorganize your life so that it is more in harmony with your dreams and desires?

2. What three new habits, if done daily, would do the most to bring you closer to your dream?

3. What one single habit, if done every day, would most transform your life?

4. What habits could you eliminate from your life to create more productivity, more time, or more energy?

9

Pivot People

There are two questions that we have to ask ourselves. The first is "Where am I going?" and the second is "Who will go with me?"

—HOWARD THURMAN, THEOLOGIAN

AT THE age of sixteen, Venus was living on the streets of Baltimore, Maryland.

"I was living on the mean street," she recalled, "and I really do mean *mean* street. I come from a background of violence, a history of addicts . . . this whole world of drugs, prostitutes, pimps, police. I was eating at a trash can, literally sleeping in piss and beer on my street corner in Baltimore, when I prayed. And it was a great simple prayer: 'God, please help me.'"

The answer to her prayer came in the form of Miss Judy Mae Francis, a teacher at her school. One day Miss Francis—Nanna to Venus—gave her a warm meal, cleaned her up, and dropped her off at school—no questions asked.

The kindness struck a chord in Venus, and she began to spend more time with Miss Francis, cleaning blackboards, then reading.

When Miss Francis got her to write down her thoughts in fragments and snippets of poetry, Miss Francis typed them up and submitted them to an NAACP competition.

Venus won.

"The winning of the contest wasn't a big deal for me," she said. "The real eye-opener was realizing what Miss Francis had done for me. She was a math teacher. She wasn't an English teacher. But she had turned herself into a resource on my behalf, so I could see me as wise. She gave me the tools to have a voice. She put her love on me that I didn't have to earn or prove or pay for. It was in that real-ization that I had my very first new thought: Miss Francis sees me differently than I see me. Miss Francis sees me as somebody who matters. If I could see me as how she sees me, then maybe I could do something with my life."

Miss Francis sees me differently. It was a powerful insight. At that point, no one in Venus's family—in her entire bloodline—had even finished high school. But now, empowered by the kindness of a teacher, Venus set out to change that.

Fourteen years later, Doctor Venus Opal Reese graduated from Stanford University with a second master's degree and a PhD. And she has kept on going. She has appeared in *Forbes* and was featured in *Ebony* magazine as one of four millionaires who had made their money from their passion.

Dr. Venus's journey to success is an inspiring story of how it's possible to pivot from even the most difficult conditions. But it's also a testimony to another essential concept of pivot momentum: *No one pivots alone.*

▶● PIVOT POINT: **No one pivots alone.**

2

Your Pivot People

When I became the CEO of one of the world's largest personal growth companies, I was clear on my vision and purpose: to grow our ability to change the lives of millions of people through our fabulous courses and camps. What I wasn't clear about was how to do that better than it had been done before.

I made my vision well-known in the company, but I did not seek out the collaboration of my leadership team to discuss, debate, and create clear plans for the execution of that vision. I thought that if everyone knew the overall mission, things would just flow in that direction.

I couldn't have been more wrong. I soon found that the vision was not being well-executed because I wasn't communicating it. I didn't want anyone to know that I didn't have complete clarity myself, so I kept to myself. It was a rude and costly awakening but one that I needed to experience in order to learn the lesson that *pivoting is not a solo sport*.

Until that time, I'd done many things by myself. I'd practiced law alone. I'd built a career and business mostly alone. I tended to feel that I didn't always fit into a team, and as a result I had become a sort of one-man show. I was effective, but I now realized that to affect millions of lives, which was my dream, I needed to move beyond that. I had to move from being a "solo-preneur" to someone who collaborated. The future of my dream rested on my ability to work well and be part of an unstoppable team.

There is no doubt that whatever your vision might be or become, you will need and want the assistance of others. Whether you plan to start a business, write a book, or become an artist, doctor, lawyer, or mechanic, you're going to need other people. Those others might be your family, your friends, your partners in business, or your co-workers. They could be your neighbors, your boss, or the friend of a friend of a friend.

Regardless of who it is, you'll never pivot alone. And that's not a drawback; it's a benefit.

▶• PIVOT POINT: **Change is a team sport.**

In fact, your "pivot people" can offer several benefits.

You'll gain more clarity. It's almost impossible to gain perfect clarity alone. Sometimes you're simply too close to something. Your vision becomes tainted, and you simply can't see that your idea for hamburger-flavored ice cream isn't the million-dollar concept you thought it was.

You'll save. Pivot people can save you time, energy, money, and, most of all, heartache. Express your vision to others often, and seek out opportunities to share, help, and collaborate, and you'll discover shortcuts, avoid pitfalls, and get through your pivot faster and with fewer setbacks than you ever could alone.

You'll contribute. Perhaps the most important part of pivot people is not what they can do for you but how *you* can help *them*. It's easy to feel adrift during times of change, and sometimes helping someone else is the best way to help yourself.

The Virtuous Cycle of Pivots and People

Have you ever dreamed of doubling your income?

Of course you have. Haven't we all? When I stand in front of audiences and ask that question, hands shoot up across the room. We've all dreamed of doubling our income.

I've asked that question of audiences around the world, and after the hands shoot up, I tell people to forget about it. Doubling your income is what I call "2x thinking" (I pronounce it "two-ex thinking"), and it's a recipe for more of what you don't want.

Confused? I'll tell you what I explain to audiences: 2x thinking is a mind-set of struggle. It's the thinking that says, "If I could just double my income, my problems would go away."

But there's a problem with that. The 2x mind-set leads to a simple question: *What can I do?* Can I work harder? Read a book? Multi-task? Squeeze more hours out of the day? Work eight days a week? Those are all solutions that lead you to simply doing the same thing, only harder.

And if simply working twice as hard was going to deliver what you wanted, wouldn't you know it by now?

Instead, I propose 10x thinking ("ten-ex thinking").

The 10x mind-set is different. When we think of multiplying our income by ten, we know we can't do that just by working harder. We know we can't do it in the life framework we currently have. We know we can't do it alone. 10x thinking, then, leads us to ask a different question: *Who can help me?*

That's a very powerful question. It leads us to seek help. Which then allows us to dream bigger. Which requires more help. It's a virtuous cycle of growth that can be scaled up as far as we want it to.

Nicole Brandon, who knows more than a little about both success and setbacks, used the power of trusting others to take her career to an entirely new level.

Nicole is an actress, bestselling author, and award-winning dancer who began her dance career at the age of seven, winning hundreds of dance competitions and appearing in such theater productions as *A Chorus Line* and *Fiddler on the Roof*, and films like *The Flamingo Kid* and *Mr. Saturday Night*.

After nearly dying in a car accident and being told she would never walk again, however, she faced a long road to recovery. Yet just a year later, she was hiking the Great Wall of China and performing as an acrobat.

But for all her accomplishments, setbacks, and successes, her greatest challenge still remained. "The one element I had never had in my life until that point was a team. I'd done everything on my own. Even as an entrepreneur, I'd done everything alone."

When she was invited to perform with Diavolo, an American

dance company, Nicole found herself in new territory. Performing with Diavolo had been a dream since she was a teenager, but the company's blend of dance, acrobatics, and gymnastics called for training that was a stretch even for Nicole. Running blindfolded through obstacles and flying twenty-five feet through the air in complete darkness to be caught by another performer revealed something completely new to the seasoned performer.

"Every time I jumped, I knew I would never hit the ground. It gave me the opportunity to say, 'What would it be like if someone caught me? What would it be like if someone supported me? What would it be like if other people were there?' The lesson in trust and teamwork was what I needed."

Inspired by the power of teamwork, Nicole forged further. She now travels the world as a sought-after speaker, writer, and humanitarian.

As Nicole and a multitude of others have discovered, **to pivot successfully means to involve others.** You'll need advice. You'll need support—emotionally, perhaps financially, maybe spiritually. If you want to pivot and you don't involve your spouse, for example, your pivot will be immensely more difficult.

Even if you're a loner or an introvert, there will be people involved in your pivot. Even if your pivot is just to sit in a remote cabin and write a manifesto, you'll need other people to help you get there. I call them "pivot people," and they are anyone who has a significant impact on your plans for reinvention. I group pivot people into three categories: stakeholders, mentors, and collaborators. Each brings something different, but essential, to your pivot.

1. Stakeholders

Primary role: committed support

Thomas Tadlock was broke. He had just been fired from his job as a personal trainer when his wife gave birth to their first son. With only a maternity-leave income to support them, Thomas regrouped. "The personal training business was just wiping me out with all the hours I had to train just to be able to sustain our living," he said.

Instead, he decided to try a group approach to training and started a fitness boot camp where he could train many people at once.

It was, in Thomas's words, "a horrible failure. I spent nine months doing the best I could to get as many people enrolled and I only got fourteen members, which only brought in about $1,000 to $1,500 a month—which in Orange County, California, was not nearly enough to even pay our rent. We were in the red almost every month, and I just didn't know what to do. I was feeling absolute desperation."

Things changed for Thomas when he received a ticket to our Millionaire Mind Intensive. There he discovered the Quantum Leap program, an accelerated success training program that he was sure could help his business.

Quantum Leap is a wide-ranging, intensive curriculum for people committed to creating financial freedom. Courses in the program such as Life Directions, Guerrilla Business School, Never Work Again, and Enlightened Warrior Training help students discover immediate and long-term benefits in all areas of their lives, from financial and spiritual to relationships and health.

Thomas took them all. "Every single course just took me to another level. But the challenges—it required more of my time than ever before. I was working about thirteen to fifteen hours a day, and the first year of my son's life, I wasn't in it. I was in the office down the hall, and I was getting up early and going to bed really late, just trying to spend every last hour that I could to build my business and my company."

Those were trying times for Thomas and his wife. But they paid off.

"I went to every single course, applied everything that I learned, and it took my business from fourteen members to over fifteen hundred members; from one location to four locations, including a contract on-location boot camp at British Petroleum, making it the single largest indoor fitness boot camp in all of Orange County, California. And then I sold the company and took all the money that I made and invested it."

Just over two years after his first MMI program, Thomas and his family had gone from almost broke to fully financially free.

But what does Thomas credit his success to? "I can definitely tell you that what I had going for me was just an amazing relationship with my wife before it even began. It was just beyond rock-solid. We're soul mates, and we just love and trust each other more than anything, and the most important thing in our lives is our happiness. And that's what it was all for, and every time it started to get hard, that's what I would keep reminding her of."

Thomas's wife was a stakeholder in his pivot. Someone with a vested interest in his success. Though your neighbor's life might not change much if you fail to pivot, a stakeholder has some skin in the game. If you succeed, that person succeeds, too. And with a new baby and bills to pay, Thomas's wife needed him to succeed as badly as he did.

▶● PIVOT POINT: **Stakeholders are people whose own lives will be affected by your pivot.**

Your stakeholders include your spouse and immediate family and any other dependents. They may also include business partners. Anyone who will suffer if you don't pivot successfully is a stakeholder, and you need to work with them in three specific ways:

Share early and often. Your neighbors or work colleagues don't need to know about your pivot, but your stakeholders sure do. They need to be insiders from the start and treated as if their own money, time, and energy are on the line—because they are. Pivoting consumes stakeholders in its own way, and it's important to honor that.

Ask for committed support. You can't expect your spouse to support you by default; it's important to ask. First of all, it's respectful, and second, it's establishing, out loud, a commitment to supporting what you're trying to do. Assuming you have stakeholder support is a pivot problem waiting to happen.

Show gratitude. Don't forget that the harder your pivot gets, the harder it is on your stakeholders, too. You might have to take time away from family. You might ride a few emotional waves. There may be sacrifices. It's important that you acknowledge the crucial role that stakeholders play just by their unwavering support.

In describing his pivot, Thomas gives enormous credit to his wife for her support. "I'm just so lucky that my wife trusted me enough to be able to give me the space that I needed." Part of the reason she was able to is that Thomas treated her as a stakeholder.

What can you do if you don't have stakeholder support? Ask a key question: "What would have to happen for you to support me in this change?" Even reluctant stakeholders can become powerful allies if you make them part of the process.

2. Mentors

Primary role: provision of wisdom

Mentors are people who have wisdom, resources, or skills that you don't but that can help your pivot. They might have experience in an industry. They might be accomplished entrepreneurs. They could be spiritual advisers, coaches, counselors, business owners, or subject experts. Whatever they are, mentors can be critical allies on the road to your pivot.

Just as Miss Francis provided unconditional love and insight to Dr. Venus and T. Harv Eker provided business mentoring to me, mentors can provide you with something you don't have access to. It could be advice, it might be connections. It could be insight or support. But in each case a mentor has the power to open doors—in the mind, the spirit, or the physical world—that you might not be able to open on your own.

The best mentors, of course, are people who have already successfully done what you want to do. If you want to start a software company, for example, find someone who's already done it. If you want to write a book, find an author. If you want to reduce your body fat, find someone who's done it.

▶● PIVOT POINT: Mentors are people who have wisdom, resources, or skills that can help your pivot.

Some important considerations when choosing mentors:

1. **Note the key word *successfully*.** Finding someone who's failed at starting a coaching business may teach you something, but *that person is not a mentor.* A mentor is someone who's succeeded.
2. **They need to have done the work.** Getting weight loss advice from someone who's never been overweight isn't as helpful as learning from someone who's gone from obese to healthy. A mentor is someone who's done the work.
3. **You can have many mentors.** Your pivot might require input from many people, across many skills or professions. You don't need to find someone who's started a plumbing supply business in Topeka in order to start a plumbing supply business in Topeka.
4. **They come in many forms.** You can learn from people who are dead. You can learn from fictitious people. You can learn from people whom you've never spoken to. *Mentorship is about studying success.*

▶• PIVOT POINT: Mentorship is about studying success, and that
can take many forms.

How do you find mentors? For Keith Leon, who pivoted to become a bestselling author, the secret was *don't be needy*. He had tried
reaching out to successful people for advice in the past but had met
with limited success.

"Before, when I was reaching out to mentors, I felt like I needed
them to get me to my next level, so I was showing up in front of
them needy. If you're in a relationship with someone who's needy,
what do you want to do? Get away from them as quickly as possible,
and that's the result I was having."

As Keith was interviewing successful people for his book, however, he realized that not only was he creating content for a book, but
they were the same people who could help him sell it.

"I had seen a handful of them go from e-book to *New York Times*
bestseller, and I figured I'd reach out and ask them if they would
share (a) how they did it, (b) when would they be willing to teach
me, and (c) how much would they charge me to teach me. They
all shared with me everything they personally knew about selling
books successfully. None of them charged me a dime for this. I just
showed up as a doer instead of a talker, with a great project, and
was willing to ask for the support. I just took great notes and imple-
mented what they taught me."

That realization changed everything.

"In one year's time my life had completely pivoted," Keith recalled. "I now had a bestseller and the three mentors I had always
dreamed of having."

Likewise, the author and speaker Greg Montana found a willing
mentor in the speaker and bestselling author Blair Singer using a
unique approach that focused on respect and a willingness to exe-
cute.

"I will take five minutes of your time, *once*," Greg recalled telling
him. "I'll spend two of those minutes telling you what my goals are

and what I've done. You give me three minutes of coaching, and I will make sure you're off the phone in five minutes. You tell me anything I need to do, and I'll do it. If I do what you tell me to do, I have a right to call you back and have five more minutes of your time. If I don't do what you tell me to do, I have no right to call you back."

Singer's answer? "Let's do it."

3. Peers

Primary role: collaboration

There's a world of people out there who can contribute to your pivot but who aren't stakeholders or mentors. They don't depend on your success, and they don't necessarily have the experience you need for your pivot, but they can play an important role nonetheless. I call these people your peers.

I use the word *peers* to describe more than just people you work with. They could be colleagues at work, friends, professionals from other fields, like-minded pivoters, or entrepreneurs at the same stage you are. None of them alone can transform your pivot. But put them together? That's a whole different story, and it's exactly what happens when you create a mastermind with your peers.

A *mastermind*, by my definition, is two or more people coming together in harmony to create definite plans for the achievement of a desired end, and it's the best way to work with peers.

> ▶● PIVOT POINT: A mastermind is two or more people coming together in harmony to create definite plans for the achievement of a desired end.

Typically, masterminds are meetings that run for set amounts of time, where each participant is given time to talk about his or her desire, purpose, issue, challenge, and so on, and their fellow participants brainstorm solutions, ideas, and next steps.

Some of the most powerful and successful entrepreneurs, business owners, artists, musicians, and even employees have utilized the power of the mastermind. Steve Jobs and Steve Wozniak came together in 1976 to collaborate on what became the world's first personal computer.

The collaboration of John Lennon, Paul McCartney, George Harrison, and Richard Starkey, otherwise known as the Beatles, was a prime example of the synergistic results of a mastermind. Each Beatle was clearly talented in his own right, but none ever accomplished as an individual the same volume of critically acclaimed music that they wrote, played, and produced as a group.

Why are masterminds so effective? First, they diversify our thinking. To create new results in your life, you must think differently and act differently than you have before. Or, as my grandmother would have said, if what you are looking for was where you have been looking, you probably would have found it by now. Likewise, if who you were hanging around with was going to influence you to greater and greater success, chances are that that result would have become evident before now.

Second, it has been said that the coming together of multiple minds with a common purpose creates a "third" mind of "infinite intelligence." That is the mastermind. The mastermind becomes greater than any of the parts themselves.

There is no one method or procedure to conduct a mastermind. The mystery and miracle of it is that the mastermind takes on a life of its own. But here are four basic principles that maximize the potential of a group:

1. **Choose the participants carefully.** In the early twentieth century, when Henry Ford toured the eastern United States in his company's cars on a series of promotional camping trips, he chose for his company the likes of the inventor Thomas Edison, the rubber magnate Harvey Firestone, and the renowned naturalist John Burroughs as companions. You don't need to have famous people in your group, but

diversity and a common focus on excellence will always deliver results.

2. **Maintain a regular connection.** A casual association will produce casual results. It's essential that your mastermind be in regular contact, which means weekly if not daily meetings or calls until each participant has clear plans.

3. **Distribute accountability.** Someone must organize the meetings, keep the minutes, facilitate the discussion, and move the agenda forward. It usually works best to rotate the responsibilities so that each member takes a turn at these vital functions and each may lead and also be led in the process.

4. **Know that "givers gain."** There is an old saying, "You will receive only that which you are first willing to give." For a mastermind to be fruitful, the participants should come to the table prepared to give more than they take. For a mastermind to be successful, there must be a yin and yang, a harmony of giving and receiving. Perhaps not surprisingly, the more one gives freely, without expectation, the more that person actually does receive to support his or her purpose.

An effective mastermind is exponential in nature, with the group becoming something more than the sum of its parts. Mahatma Gandhi created probably the largest and most effective mastermind in history, helping more than 200 million people to cooperate in mind and body, and in a spirit of harmony, for the specific purpose of peacefully taking back the sovereignty of India from the British.

You Are Your Own Curator

According to Jewish law, at the age of thirteen a boy becomes a man and is accountable for his actions—he becomes a *bar mitzvah* and a full member of the Jewish community.

At the time I became a teenager that meant attending Hebrew school regularly to prepare for my bar mitzvah ceremony. Hebrew school would teach me, among other things, how to read from the Torah in front of all my friends and family and my local community.

Reading from the Torah is no easy task for anyone, especially not for a teen boy who'd rather be doing almost anything but studying. The rabbi of my synagogue, a lifelong student of the Torah, was an older man, and we were cut from different cloth. I was a thirteen-year-old kid who loved sports and my friends. He was older, more disciplined, and prone to criticize. I cut Hebrew school a lot.

I'd tell my parents I was going and then go to the movies or spend my time doing anything but preparing. To say my Hebrew was not strong would be an understatement.

About a month before my bar mitzvah ceremony, things were reaching a bit of a crisis. Our rabbi was deeply concerned about my lack of preparation. He would call our home at odd hours to discuss my progress (or lack of it), and a month before the ceremony he finally met with my parents to break the news: Your son is not ready to become a bar mitzvah. After all the preparations and expense, the rabbi was essentially getting ready to pull the plug on my ceremony.

That was not great news for my parents. Becoming a bar mitzvah is a big deal. My parents had rented a venue for the celebration, where we'd feed everyone a fine meal at a cost per head that was far more than my parents were easily able to afford. The Sabbath date for my ceremony had been booked long in advance—at that time, only one boy per Saturday was bar mitzvahed. All my relatives would be there to hear me recite from the Torah, including my grandparents, who were from the "old country" and spoke Hebrew themselves. Canceling the ceremony would be expensive, embarrassing, and disappointing.

About a week after the rabbi's visit we received a phone call telling us that he had died suddenly. I steeled myself to go to the temple to meet our new rabbi.

He turned out to be a young man, very different from the old leader of our temple. He was kind and open, and he inspired me. He told me there was a lot of work to do, a lot of studying, but he believed in me and told me I could do it. And for the first time I felt motivated.

I put my head down and studied. I met with the new rabbi regularly. I learned my section of the Torah—which in that day meant reading the actual vowelless Torah, not the phonetic English punctuation—and I learned numerous prayers that would be part of my ceremony.

And in the end? I did it, and did it well. It wasn't perfect, but it felt amazing.

That was a pivotal moment for me. Not just because I'd become a bar mitzvah but because of what I'd discovered about myself. I had learned about self-discipline and about focus. About what I could accomplish if I put my head down and did the work. In that moment I realized that I was much more, and much more confident, than I believed I had been.

The contrast between the two rabbis was profound. Whereas one criticized, the other coached. Whereas one made me feel small, the other helped me see potential. And in the end, whereas one couldn't help me, the other lifted me to discover things I never knew I could do.

That pivotal motivation has shown up ever since in my life in many different ways. The tenacity and goal setting that I developed then stayed with me my whole life and are now personal traits that are among my strongest and most important. I'm goal-oriented, and I'm a "whatever it takes" person, and I learned that from my experience with the new rabbi.

You'll have both kinds of "rabbis" in your life. You'll have fans, and you'll have naysayers. You'll have prophets of both prosperity and doom. *And you get to decide which to pay attention to.*

You are the curator of the people in your life. You get to decide whom to invite to participate in the journey you're on. They, in turn, get to decide whether to join you.

Choose carefully. Because those people—whomever you gather to you on your journey—can build the momentum you need to pivot or can tear it down, word by word and day by day.

You can't avoid all the naysayers; they will always be there. But you can choose whether to keep them close.

You can't always have the mentors you want, but you can choose whom to ask.

You can't always have the support of your stakeholders and peers, but you can choose whether to include them.

Those simple choices can make all the difference.

▶● PIVOT POINT: **You are the curator of the people in your life.**

▶• PIVOT POINTS

> No one pivots alone.

> Change is a team sport.

> Stakeholders are people whose own lives will be affected by your pivot.

> Mentors are people who have wisdom, resources, or skills that can help your pivot.

> Mentorship is about studying success, and that can take many forms.

> A mastermind is two or more people coming together in harmony to create definite plans for the achievement of a desired end.

> You are the curator of the people in your life.

▶•PIVOTAL QUESTIONS

1. Who are the stakeholders in your pivot?

2. Can you identify someone (you don't need to know him or her personally) who has successfully done something similar to your vision?

3. Who do you know who would make a great mastermind member?

4. Are you open to feedback and collaboration? Are you sure?

10

Resilience

I have missed more than nine thousand shots in my career. I have lost almost three hundred games. On twenty-six occasions I have been entrusted to take the game-winning shot, and I missed. I have failed over and over and over again in my life. And that is why I succeed.

—MICHAEL JORDAN

ABRAHAM LINCOLN is often cited as an example of someone who rose above a daunting series of failures. Over the course of more than four decades, the future president experienced a string of painful setbacks.

Lincoln's mother died when he was just nine, his sister when he was nineteen. As an adult, he failed in business and then lost a bid for the state legislature the following year. That same year he lost his job and failed to get into law school. A year later he went bankrupt in another failed business. In 1835, he was engaged to be married, but his sweetheart died. The next year, he had a nervous breakdown. In the following years, he would lose bids for the state legislature and Congress twice, then carry on and fail to win a place in the

175

Senate twice. At his party's national convention he got fewer than a hundred votes for the vice presidential nomination. And of his four children, only one would live to adulthood.

At first glance, it's a sad but ultimately triumphant tale—despite the setbacks and tragedies, Lincoln went on to become one of the greatest U.S. presidents in history.

What the simplified "Lincoln failure" stories don't tend to focus on, however, is the successes in between. Lincoln was elected company captain of the Illinois militia. He was elected to the Illinois state legislature twice and to Congress. He received his license to practice law and went on to make partner. He received (but declined) appointments as secretary and then governor of the Oregon Territory. He was admitted to practice law in the U.S. Supreme Court.

Though the first story, the "Lincoln failures," is heartbreaking, the second reads like the path to success of a born politician. *But they're both about the same person.* Almost the entire time Lincoln was failing, he was also succeeding. He didn't lead a disastrous life and then wake up one day as president. He bounced back from each setback. He built momentum despite, and at times because of, his setbacks.

In a word, Lincoln was *resilient*. It's how he built momentum, and you can do the same thing in your own life—you can use resilience to make steady progress toward your goals.

Whatever vision you have for your life, you can be assured that it'll come with some adversity. Even the best-laid plans are subject to mistakes, accidents, economics, and the winds of fate. Like Lincoln's, the story of your life could be told in two ways—one of adversity, one of triumph.

But the true story of your life, just like the true story of Abraham Lincoln, contains both tragedy and triumph. It's a tale of facing adversity, then rising above it. It's a story of *resilience*.

Keys to Resilience

Resilience isn't just about being strong—although it helps to be. And resilience isn't just about surviving setbacks—although there will be times you have to. Resilience is about being strong, taking a beating, and then coming back as something greater. When you're resilient, you become like a spring, meeting an opposing force and bouncing back again.

Producing your first theater production to disappointing reviews—and then starting work on play number two? That's resilience.

Launching a new product to dismal sales—and then stepping up your marketing efforts to turn it around? That's resilience.

Resilience isn't just about facing adversity, it's taking that adversity and using it to fuel your forward motion—it's about taking a setback or disappointment or failure and using it to move further. To, in other words, create momentum.

▶● PIVOT POINT: Resilience is the ability to experience setbacks or failures and use them to create momentum.

Every pivoter—in this book and anywhere else that I know of—has faced adversity. The ones who were resilient, who bounced back stronger and wiser, are the ones you hear of and read about. The ones without resilience simply never came back. Resilience is the yeast in the pivot recipe; you need it in order to rise.

Perhaps the most enticing and exciting aspect of resilience, though, is that it's a skill you can build. As Dr. Venus said, "Anytime someone says adversity—to me that's an opinion. I think adversity is a perception—probably your best teacher; it's probably the opportunity for you to step up and grow."

How can you seize that opportunity and continue to build momentum? There are three keys to resilience, each of them something you can take control of.

Key 1: Change Your Story

Martin Seligman, who has been called the father of positive psychology, has spent decades studying optimism and pessimism and notes that our "explanatory style"—how we explain setbacks to ourselves—makes all the difference in creating optimism (and therefore our resilience). Seligman describes three elements of the explanatory style of optimists, which are useful for cultivating resilience in your pivot.

Imagine, for example, that you've decided to start a small yoga studio. After some searching, you find an affordable space that will let you run classes in one of its rooms. You paint it. You set up a website. You spread the word on social media, put up flyers, hand out discount coupons to local stores. Your excitement grows.

You invest in a dozen yoga mats, a water cooler, and a few other essentials, and within a month after finding the space, you're ready to launch your low-risk, part-time dream business.

Opening day arrives. Your first class is scheduled for 5 P.M.—right at the end of the workday. You spend the day in nervous excitement, getting everything just right.

And no one arrives.

If your stomach just dropped a little, you're not alone. Pursuing your dream, and then having no one notice, is a horrible feeling. There's no getting around it: It sucks.

What do you do now?

Well, if you're Seligman, what you do next will depend on how you think next. It will depend on the story you tell yourself about the setback.

In Seligman's research, he found that the explanatory styles of optimists and pessimists differed in three key areas.

- **Permanence.** Optimists tend to see setbacks as temporary, not permanent. They tend to think, *Classes will fill up once I get some momentum,* not *This will never work.*

- **Pervasiveness.** Optimists don't see setbacks as permeating their whole life. They think, *I wasn't successful with this first yoga class,* not *Everything in my life always goes wrong.*
- **Personalization.** Optimists don't assume that failures are personality flaws. They might think, *Starting a new hot yoga class on the hottest day of the summer probably wasn't the best idea,* instead of *I'm no good at business.*

Failures invite explanation. It's just part of our nature—when we experience a setback, we want to understand why. It might be unconscious, but it's unavoidable, and we use those three elements to build the story that explains why things went off the rails.

The key, however, is that our way of explaining our setbacks is, at least in part, a habit. And that means we can rewire it using rituals.

You can use your morning ritual to cultivate resilience by ensuring that you see failures as temporary, isolated to the event in question, and not character flaws. Millions of businesses have had rocky starts. It doesn't mean they were failures. If your first book sells only twenty copies, it doesn't mean your next one can't sell twenty thousand. It doesn't mean you're a bad writer.

Cultivating resilience means changing the story you tell yourself. But make no mistake—our culture's stories of "failure" are pervasive, and they can be disempowering. From our earliest days of schooling into working at most jobs, we're taught that failure is bad and that it's our own fault.

Resilience, though, requires us to see setbacks differently. You'll need to change the story you tell yourself. You'll need to see setbacks as challenges, not deal breakers. You'll need to tear apart failures, look for the parts you can control, and focus on them. *You'll need to explain the hard times differently.*

▶● PIVOT POINT: Your resilience depends on changing how you explain setbacks.

Key 2: Find the Lesson

Changing the way you explain setbacks can take you a long way. But it's also critical to learn from them. After all, you won't pivot far if you remain caught in the same cycle, facing the same setbacks over and over. You have to use resilience to break the cycle and move on.

There are two ways of doing this. The first is to simply learn to avoid the same mistakes—to be able to recognize what went wrong and avoid the same pitfall. Making mistakes is fine, but continuing to do the same thing and expecting different results is a recipe for staying right where you are instead of pivoting.

It took flight attendant turned entrepreneur Lisa Lent a year to develop her first product, Flight Pack, and it failed. But she came back stronger than ever. She took what she learned, filled the holes, found a great partner to help her, and bounced back even higher with her million-dollar brand Oxylent. "All the lessons of life," she said. "You get to learn from them and move forward."

The second way to find the lesson is to look for insight. Sometimes a setback isn't demonstrating a mistake but offering us a piece of wisdom or a new path forward.

As a psychotherapist, Marcy Cole counseled hundreds of people on how to be great parents, and she always assumed she would be a mother herself. But she was heartbroken to find out she could not conceive.

"Our reinventions of life are often inspired by the challenges and sometimes the heartbreaks we face. The inability to have children was mine," she explained. "While periodic waves of grief would wash over me, my awareness of the slew of women in my world who are also childless, by choice or circumstance, became striking and palpable. I noticed those who were childless by choice birthing other visions and projects of great meaning and contribution. I also witnessed others struggling with trying to find solace, peace, and acceptance with this unexpected, wanted, or wished-for reality— trying to find their calling, legacy, and find fulfillment in their lives."

Marcy's journey eventually led to creating Childless Mothers Connect, an online forum where women without children can share their trials, triumphs, resources, services, and celebrations with one another. This was also the catalyst for her 2011 launch of Childless Mothers Adopt, an organization founded on the mission of advocating for orphaned children by connecting them with childless single women, men, couples, and partners via adoption, foster care, or mentorship.

"The decision to turn my own disappointment into a calling that can touch so many lives in a positive way has healed my heart and catapulted my life's work to a whole new level of possibility, satisfaction, and impact," Marcy explained. "I am clear now and so very grateful for all that has happened *and* not happened in my life; and I am certain that the best is yet to come."

Marcy's inability to have children of her own wasn't a mistake. It wasn't a pitfall she could simply avoid in order to pivot. But she was able to find the wisdom in her situation and turn it into a powerful mission. Her resilient comeback healed her and positively affected the lives of many, many others.

Discovering the lessons of a setback and learning to avoid future ones winds the spring of resilience, so you can bounce back higher and further than ever.

▶● PIVOT POINT: Every setback has a lesson that can help you pivot.

Key 3: Move Your Body

What if I told you there was a miracle treatment that could do all of the following:

- Help prevent heart disease, cancer, and dementia.
- Improve your sleep and concentration and help you form new brain cells.

- Reduce your depression, stress, and anxiety.
- Reduce fatigue and improve your work productivity.
- Decrease bone fractures and arthritis.
- Boost your mood, self-esteem, and immune system.

As an added bonus, it reduces your risk of premature death.

That miracle treatment is exercise. And not even hard exercise. You can get many of these astonishing benefits just from walking.

If there's one single thing you should include in your pivot ritual that is almost guaranteed to help you become more resilient, it's *moving your body*. Because if you're like the average person, you almost certainly aren't doing it enough.

Dr. James Levine, the director of the Mayo Clinic/Arizona State University Obesity Solutions Initiative, is the inventor of the tread-mill desk and credited with coining the phrase "Sitting is the new smoking." Levine has studied the impact of a sedentary lifestyle for years. Here's his take, in two sentences: "Sitting is more dangerous than smoking, kills more people than HIV, and is more treacherous than parachuting. We are sitting ourselves to death."

Strong words indeed. But exercise makes you more resilient, both physically and mentally. It creates a stronger spring that can take more force and bounce back harder and further.

The best part about moving your body is that it facilitates the other two keys. Heading out for a long walk, for example, can give you the space and clarity you need to work through the story you're telling yourself about a setback and find the lesson that it contains.

▶• PIVOT POINT: Exercise can make you more resilient.

These three keys combine to do one thing well: to help you *decompress* after a setback. A spring can't bounce back until you take the pressure off it. There's no way to be resilient—to bounce—unless you decompress. You need to remove the pressure of the setback, and you do that by changing your story, finding the lesson in the setback, and moving your body.

Do those three things, and you'll find your spring uncoiling, ready for the next bounce in the pivot road.

Cultivating the Resilience Habit

If you look at the components of resilience—change your story, find the lesson, move your body—they're all tasks that you need to do. You need to change your self-talk in order to shift the story you're telling yourself about setbacks and adversity. You need to seek the insight or wisdom in challenging moments. And you need to go out and move your body. No one is going to become resilient for you.

Because these are all things that need to be done by you, they're also ripe for habitualization. Can you train your mind to automatically see challenges in the right light? Can you turn exercise or some other form of activity into a *habit*?

The answer is yes, and the best way to do it, to cultivate a resilience *habit*, is to build its components into your daily ritual. For example, you can:

- Write in a journal to explore how you explain a setback in ways that aren't permanent, pervasive, or personal.
- Use a period of silence or meditation to seek the insight in a setback.
- Add an exercise component to every day. Even a walk is enough. When you face a setback, add more.

Your resilience ritual is like a pressure relief valve. When times get tough, your ritual will be something you can turn to. If you habitualize it, you won't have to think to turn to it—it will become something you do automatically.

▶● PIVOT POINT: The most resilient people have made resilience a
habit.

We're all more resilient than we realize. If you struggle with achieving resilience, I've found it's helpful to use the following exercise to uncover your "success recipe"—the common elements that exist at times when you are persistent and successful.

1. Reflect on the most important achievement in your life to date. Don't compare yourself to others; you don't need to dent the universe, just think of a time when you felt proud of what you'd accomplished.

2. In writing, describe the scene—what you did, what you accomplished, who was there, how it felt. Just use bullet points, and capture as many details as possible. Think of the time leading up to your accomplishment. What did you do? Were there obstacles to surmount? Did you have to get help? What was hard, and what was easy?

3. Look through your list of bullet points. Identify three to five things—specific attitudes, actions, resources, or people— that were most critical to your accomplishment.

If you ran a marathon, for example, you might reflect back on your friends and family cheering you on in the final difficult stretch. You might recall the coach who gave you a detailed training program to follow and the early sunrises you saw as part of your morning training runs. You might remember the songs you played in your headphones toward the end of your long runs that kept you motivated.

From your description, you might create a "success recipe list" that looks like this:

- Achieve full family support and buy-in.
- Hire a coach.
- Create a clear action plan.
- Follow a consistent morning routine.
- Develop rituals for energy.

What's fascinating about success recipes is that the things that make you successful in one endeavor are often the same things that can make you successful in others. That means that your success recipe can act as a reference point whenever you face a tough obstacle or feel the urge to give up.

Success comes from being able to outperform your problems more consistently. The way to do that is to know what makes you successful and focus on it when times get tough.

Persevere to Pivot

There was a point during my pivot when I felt stuck. I was still practicing law after almost fifteen years, although I'd been trained in several New Peaks programs. I felt as if I was slowly dying inside. I came home after one particularly tough day and said to my wife, "I need to do something different, or you're going to be a widow."

To her credit, she didn't remind me of our two mortgages or our children but instead was 100 percent supportive. I knew the next steps were up to me.

At that point, I'd done trainings with Harv Eker himself, and I knew that becoming a trainer was the next step on my path. What I didn't realize was just how challenging that step would be.

I had been given some assistant trainer opportunities with the company, but to become a full-fledged trainer, it turned out, I would have to try out for the job. I was given a four-page script and invited to the company's head office in Vancouver to deliver the sample training program in front of Harv.

I felt confident at that point and in many ways considered the tryout to be a formality. After all, I was on my path. I knew what I wanted, and I was on my way.

When I arrived at the office, however, there were three other people waiting. They each had the same script and were there for the same reason I was. I began to feel the first seeds of unease.

We were all ushered into a very small room. At the front was a long table with a video camera in front of it. The door opened, and three people came in—Harv Eker, one of his partners, and the company COO. They asked us one by one to deliver the training script.

I was just five seconds into my presentation when they stopped me and corrected my approach.

I started to speak, and seconds later they stopped me again. And again. And again. At one point Eker cut me off, saying, "Boring!" and then, moments later, called out, "You're putting me to sleep!"

I was incredibly rattled. The whole experience was surreal. During the presentation they asked me to say something about my family. At that point I'd been happily married for over fifteen years, with four amazing children, and I was so shaken by what was happening in the room that I was having trouble even remembering their names.

As the audition ended, I was pretty confident that my pivot had, too. In my mind, I'd crashed and burned and was the worst of the four of us. We went to dinner, and I was despondent and quiet. As I headed to the airport later, I remember thinking, *That's it. It's over.* It was a signal that I wasn't cut out for the job.

But despite the disastrous day, part of me knew that I *was* cut out for it. Returning to my law practice, I was reminded again that *something had to change.* So I renewed my commitment. I continued as an assistant trainer for the company and began to coach private clients and do group mentoring on the side to expand my skills. When Peaks held a New Year's party in January, I decided to attend and approach the owner again. This time, I resolved, I'd try a different approach.

The night progressed from a social cocktail hour to company awards and a dinner. After dinner, I noticed Harv standing alone and walked up to him. "Harv," I said, "I want to ask you something. Would you be willing to mentor me?"

There was a short pause. He looked me in the eye and said, "No."

No explanation. No excuse. Just "No."

Once more I flew home, uncertain and disappointed.

But I persevered. Okay, I thought, this isn't going to be easy, and it isn't going to be handed to me. If I wanted motivation, I was going to have to motivate myself. If I wanted mentoring, I was going to have to make it happen—he clearly wasn't going to. And so I continued my role as an assistant trainer and kept showing up at my law practice.

Six months later, I was still committed. I was traveling for Peaks as an assistant trainer. It was little money and not exactly my dream, but it was incremental progress. Meanwhile, I began to wind down my law practice, slowly building the bridge from my old life to my new one, all the while wondering how I was going to make it work. I had no idea, but I knew staying still wasn't an option, so I kept pushing forward.

One day I got a call in my law office. I was with a client and had forgotten to turn my phone off, so I apologized, excused myself, and answered it.

It was Eker himself. There was a Thanksgiving event in a few weeks in Singapore, and they needed a cotrainer to work with him.

I had a decision to make. It was Thanksgiving, an important family time for me, and also incredibly short notice to prepare for my first colead role. I had none of the information or scripts for the program. I would be standing in front of five thousand people in a room the size of a football field. Half the people wouldn't speak English, so there would be simultaneous translation in multiple languages. I would be putting my entire future on the line as a trainer with Peaks. If I screwed up, there would almost certainly be no second chance.

I said yes immediately.

Then I hung up the phone, sat back, and thought, *What the hell did I just do?*

At Thanksgiving, I flew to Singapore for the event as planned. Harv and I had dinner the night before, and as we spoke and prepared, he began giving me suggestions. He offered recommendations for speaking strategies. He showed me accelerated learning techniques and coached me on pacing and tonality.

That's when it hit me: The man who had practically booed me offstage just a few months earlier, rattled me to the point of forgetting my kids' names, and flatly refused to mentor me *was now coaching me in my pivot.*

The next day, I stood on a thirty-foot stage in front of thousands of people and knocked it out of the park.

When I look back on that time, one of the things I reflect on is how different things would have been if I'd given up. All my efforts to find clarity, all the struggle and uncertainty and effort—it would all have meant nothing if I'd simply walked away when things got tough.

In hindsight, each setback wasn't just an obstacle, nor was it a test. Each disappointment was in fact an opportunity to get better. When my moment arrived and I stepped up onto the stage in Singapore, I was better prepared because of the setbacks. It was the obstacles that ensured I was ready when the time came. That's how resilience works—it's like a muscle that gets bigger over time and gives you the strength and speed you need on race day, when it really matters.

Remember Teawna Pinard, who made a Big-D decision to reinvent herself when her young daughter found her balled up on the couch in tears? She learned resilience over *years* of challenges.

"I was dealing with a twenty-year crippling eating disorder. I've had many ups and downs. I've been really great financially at times, and I've also been at the bottom. I believe perseverance is the golden ticket to doing more, achieving more, and becoming more, and I believe that the only way to win in life is by sticking your butt in the seat and not leaving until after it's all over."

To a large degree, those who pivot are also those who simply don't stop. They persevere by becoming resilient to challenges and setbacks. They gradually train their minds and their bodies not only to surmount obstacles but to perform better because of them.

"Life is not about one obstacle, it's about many," Teawna noted. "Perseverance is a matter of will and endurance, and those who can stay the course through the bad situations—you know, the risky situations and those seemingly hopeless situations—will always triumph in the end."

Or, as one unknown author put it best: "Never let success go to your head. Never let failure go to your heart."

►•PIVOT POINTS

> Resilience is the ability to experience setbacks or failures and use them to create momentum.

> Your resilience depends on changing how you explain setbacks.

> Every setback has a lesson that can help you pivot.

> Exercise can make you more resilient.

> The most resilient people have made resilience a habit.

▶• PIVOTAL QUESTIONS

1. What was the last setback you faced?

2. How did you explain it? What story did you tell yourself about it?

3. Can you think of a time when you gave up or quit? How did it feel?

11

Growth

He who conquers others is strong; he who conquers himself is mighty.

—LAO-TZU, CHINESE PHILOSOPHER

BY 2010, Tim Jones, the architect I mentioned earlier, had pretty much reached rock bottom.

Two broken marriages and years of alcoholism had taken their toll on his health, his work, and his soul. "I was just a wreck," Tim said. "I mean, financially, emotionally, physically, spiritually, I was just a disaster."

With the help of Alcoholics Anonymous, Tim managed to sober up, but he was far from happy. "I was fifty-two at the time, and I didn't quite know what to do. I just knew what I didn't want to do anymore."

The turning point for Tim would come, as it has for many others, in the form of a book. In his case, the book was *Secrets of the Millionaire Mind*.

"It was October 31, Halloween," Tim recalled, "and I read it in one day. I sat down at nine o'clock in the morning, and I didn't leave my kitchen bar stool for the next nine hours.

"I noticed in the back of the book there was a number I could call to go to this event called the Millionaire Mind Intensive. I had no idea what that was. I didn't know who Harv was. I didn't know anything. But he said that if I called this number I would get two free tickets, so I did."

Six weeks later, Tim would find himself at a local convention center attending the Millionaire Mind Intensive event. That event led to others, and Tim began to slowly connect with a vision for his life and to learn increasingly more about business and personal development. Little by little, idea by idea, skill by skill, Tim changed how he thought and what he did.

Those years weren't always easy—in fact, they would at times be a roller-coaster ride for Tim. To reinvent himself, he pawned his classic guitar. Then his wedding ring. Then his car.

But he persevered. Today, not only is he still sober, but he's also a published author, and his architecture business is growing quickly. He's earning more money than he ever has. He got back his ring, guitar, and car (in that order), but best of all, he's happy. "My life is unimaginable," Tim says now. "If you saw me five years ago, you would not in your wildest dreams think that I could be sitting where I am right now. I love my life."

For all the ups and downs and the myriad things Tim did to pivot, when you trace the path of Tim's reinvention, it always leads back to one thing: the book. And he's not alone. Tim is one of many of the thousands of people I've worked with who trace the transformation in their lives back to a book. For some, it was the same book Tim read, *Secrets of the Millionaire Mind*. For others it was Napoleon Hill's classic *Think and Grow Rich*. For others it was the books of Tony Robbins, Tim Ferriss, or Deepak Chopra. The list is almost endless.

But in the end it's about the book. The book that made the difference. Tipped the scales. Awakened a long-dormant dream or, perhaps more than anything else, gave hope that *maybe I can change my life, too*. It's one of the reasons I wrote this book—in the hope that I can help you change your life for the better.

◆

Years ago, after the experience of believing I was having a heart attack and about to leave this world, I made a decision to make my life more like what I had dreamed it would be when I was a kid. It was a Big-D decision, fueled by my experience at the hospital and the resulting realization that I was deeply unhappy with my life.

Of course, I had no idea of what my new direction would be. All that I knew was that my current course wasn't taking me anywhere I wanted to go. I began questioning everything, but when it became clear that I didn't have the answers, I began reading.

Some of my early discovery tools were books such as *The Road Less Traveled* by Dr. M. Scott Peck and *Awaken the Giant Within* by Tony Robbins. I read books on stock trading and real estate; on personal development, such as Michael Mantell's *Don't Sweat the Small Stuff*; and on spirituality, such as *The Seven Day Mental Diet* by Emmet Fox.

During this period, my friend Sandy handed me a copy of *Secrets of the Millionaire Mind*—the same book that would begin Tim's transformation. I didn't read it right away—the title seemed to be focused on something that wasn't all that important to me—but eventually I did crack it open and begin reading. I read it and then read it again. By the time three months had passed, I had read the book ragged. It wasn't just about money or becoming wealthy but was focused on the inner workings of the mind and the "thermostat" setting that controls our decisions about money and success. It was about money, but . . . it wasn't. It was, I realized, about *everything*.

Eventually my buddy dragged me to the Peaks seminar that is a companion to the book, the Millionaire Mind Intensive. I couldn't have anticipated what happened, but something shifted for me during the program. I realized that there was a huge part of me that I was unaware of and a huge part of my life that I was not yet living. My mind was blown wide open.

It was that training program that marked the beginning of my journey with Peaks and my pivot from an unhappy, unhealthy attorney to a program trainer and eventually a CEO. The program was a mind-opening, emotional experience for me. I was intro-duced to ways of seeing my life and the world that were entirely new, yet resonated with me so profoundly that I knew I would never be the same.

One of my most vivid memories is the sense of humility it gave me. I realized that I had so far to go and there was so much for me to learn. I had barely scratched the surface of what there was to know in life. I was humbled but at the same time incredibly empowered, and in that moment I made a commitment that I would continue my learning.

At that point I had been a lawyer for many years. I'd finished my education. I'd passed my bar exams. School had been great, make no mistake—I'd met my future wife, gotten my law degree, built a career. But it was something I saw as both functional and *over*. I had no intention of going back.

That weekend at MMI, I saw things differently for the first time. A journey that had begun with something as simple as a book had ended with a decision: Not only did I want to become a student again, but I wanted to become a *lifelong* student.

Every Pivot Is a Story of Growth

My commitment to constant improvement was a pivotal moment and a Big-D decision that has truly defined the rest of my life. And I'm not alone. Consider, for example:

- Di Riseborough's decision to face, and then forgive, the man who brutally murdered her grandmother.
- Keith Leon's choice to let go of "the plan" so he could pivot after a failed product launch.
- Kristina Paider's choice to face her fear so she could live her dream life.
- Barbara Niven's pivot to become an actress despite the limitations of being a single mother.

- Marie's decision to take the first steps and start her animal rescue facility.
- Kevin Ward's reinvention as a trainer and coach.
- Dr. Venus's rise from the streets to become an inspirational leader and entrepreneur.

Every one of these stories, like all the others in this book, is wildly different yet fundamentally the same. Each is a story of growth. Find someone who has pivoted, and you've found someone who has made a decision to grow. Whether it's to gain the knowledge of a new industry, to understand themselves better, to build new habits, or to let go of fear or past hurts, every single person who pivots grows.

The same decision is before you now. *To pivot is to grow.* Are you willing to commit to personal growth?

▶● PIVOT POINT: **To pivot is to grow.**

The Growth Exchange

Growth is never free.

Yes, it may come at no charge. But it's never free. Personal growth is an exchange. In order to grow, you must give something. In return, you gain the knowledge, insight, freedom, vision, or peace that comes from having grown.

There are three forms of exchange in the growth "equation." If you expect to grow, you must offer at least one of these in return:

- Time.
- Money.
- Emotion.

Each one is an investment. It's a willing gift of something you have in exchange for a return. That return is growth and, as a result, *momentum.* The more you grow, the faster you build momentum in your reinvention.

▶• PIVOT POINT: The more you grow, the faster you build momentum.

Time

Hear the word *investment*, and you'll almost certainly think *money*. But not only is money not the only form of investment, it might be the least important when it comes to your pivot. In fact, believing that you need to spend a lot of money to pivot is a shortcut to never starting.

Some of the best ways to educate yourself and grow are free. You can find millions of books for free through your library. And now you can do much of what you'd previously have done in a library without leaving your home.

Through the wonder of online learning, you can study under some of the greatest minds of our time, at some of the greatest schools in the world, with nothing more than the Internet and a willingness to grow. From Yale and Harvard to MIT and Berkeley, the list of open courses that are available to anyone willing to sign up is growing steadily. Sites such as the Khan Academy offer a "free, world-class education for anyone, anywhere."

Want to start a business? You can learn the entire content of an MBA program for free by reading books such as *The Personal MBA*. But why worry about the MBA? You can take any number of online entrepreneurial programs and connect with other like-minded en-trepreneurs around the world.

All these things can be done for free. All they require is your time.

Money

Some of the most profound teachings in the world are free. From the libraries full of great books written over the centuries to online courses and the mentorship of wise people, you can make never-ending growth part of your entire life without spending a cent.

But you can do it a lot faster if you're also willing to invest financially.

When I spoke with Kevin Ward, who'd gone from earning $800 in his first launch to $75,000 in his coaching and training business for real estate professionals, he was still absolutely committed to his own growth.

Recall that Kevin had started his pivot with growth. "I had stopped investing in myself," he said, and it was an insight that changed his future. Kevin started small, reading books on personal growth and eventually attending seminars. And now? He's spent over $70,000 on his own personal growth *in the last twelve months*.

Money is a growth multiplier.

- You can borrow an inspirational book from the library, but when you buy it, you get to keep it, make notes in it, and revisit it as often and for as long as you like.
- You can buy the book and read it, but when you attend the transformational lectures and programs of the personal growth authors of our time, you get even more from the same content. You build relationships and discover a whole new level of personal growth.
- You can contact someone who's done what you want to do—an entrepreneur, a writer, an athlete. But when you travel to meet him or her in person, you reach a whole new level of commitment and momentum and discover new opportunities that might have taken years to do without that travel expense.
- You can meet someone once. But when you pay a coach to regularly hold you accountable to your plans, you can build momentum at an accelerated rate.

Money is a growth multiplier. It accelerates and magnifies growth to get you better results faster. And it often means you're not alone. The more you spend on your personal development, the more time you'll spend with other people, the more you'll collaborate, the more you'll learn, and the more momentum you'll build.

The beautiful thing about investing financially is that there's an entry point for every budget. Your personal growth spending is scalable, too—as you earn more, you can spend more and grow more.

The key is to start. Education should be part of your ritual: How much can you afford each month? Decide, and set that amount of money aside. You can increase it later, but don't let Kevin's daunting $70,000 scare you off. Remember that at one point he was reading books in his rented room.

The more you grow, the more you grow; money is momentum in dollar form.

Do you have to invest financially to grow? No. But if you're serious about pivoting, you need to grow. And if you're serious about growing, you can do it faster by spending.

▶● PIVOT POINT: **Money is a growth multiplier.**

Emotions

Another investment you can make that does not require risking money is to invest emotionally. Many aspects of pivoting—in case you haven't noticed—are about stretching yourself emotionally. For example:

- Doing the work of letting go of the past is an emotional investment.
- Having an honest discussion with your partner about your vision for the first time and asking for his or her support is an emotional investment.
- Sharing your writing with the world is an emotional investment.

- Contacting a stranger to ask for help is an emotional investment.
- Performing a song you wrote at a local café's open-mic night is an emotional investment.
- Changing a long-held belief is an emotional investment.

None of these things requires money. Most don't even require much time. But they do require the guts to do them. They're an emotional stretch, but they also do incredible things for your momentum.

- If you can share one story, or song, you can share more.
- If you can approach one stranger, you can approach more.
- If you can change your mind once, you can do it again.
- If you can do anything once—you can do it again.

And there's momentum: your feet moving, your life changing, your vision coming closer. Just like that.

Where to Invest?

No one growth investment is necessarily better than another. Each return you desire might demand a different type of exchange. Sometimes all three working in tandem is best. And sometimes the one you want to give the least is the one needed the most. Most pivots require at least some of each. Your pivot will have its own blend, but make no mistake: It will require growth.

▶● PIVOT POINT: Sometimes the investment you least *want* to make is the one you most *need* to make.

But where should you make your investment of time, money, and emotions? Here are three key areas.

Reading

For the lowest risk and the cheapest price, reading is a favorite start-ing place. I can say, without question, that books have changed my life. The simple act of reading a free book that a friend handed me changed the course of my future—all for the price tag of an open mind and a few comfortable hours in a favorite chair.

If you're looking for a starting point for books to build momen-tum in your pivot, let me suggest the following list:

Secrets of the Millionaire Mind by T. Harv Eker
The Road Less Traveled by M. Scott Peck
Awaken the Giant Within by Anthony Robbins
Think and Grow Rich by Napoleon Hill
The Untethered Soul by Michael A. Singer
Don't Sweat the Small Stuff by Michael Mantell
The Power of Now by Eckhart Tolle
The Alchemist by Paulo Coelho
Karmic Management by Geshe Michael Roach and Lama
    Christie McNally
The Other F Word by Juliana Ericson
Start with Why by Simon Sinek
The Seven Spiritual Laws of Success by Deepak Chopra
Autobiography of a Yogi by Paramahansa Yogananda
Delivering Happiness by Tony Hsieh
Rich Dad Poor Dad by Robert Kiyosaki with Sharon Lechter
Outwitting the Devil by Napoleon Hill
The Seven Day Mental Diet by Emmet Fox

Most you can read for free via your library. Some are available online for free as well. Regardless, each is a treasure trove of growth.

Training

I can't imagine how I would have grown enough to pivot without the many workshops, courses, and training programs I took when I began my reinvention.

The higher level of accountability, the commitment, and the heightened energy level of a room full of like-minded people are just the starting points for the amazing growth experience of a seminar. Add to that the relationships that can be built and the relief of discovering you're not alone, and training programs are an extraordinary growth opportunity.

You can find more information on New Peaks training programs at www.newpeaks.com.

People

Humility is powerful. At times, the best possible growth choice is simply to decide, "I can't get there without help."

Although the "pivot people" from Chapter 9 are an essential part of your pivot, there may come a time when you need to invest in professional help to further your growth.

A coach is someone who can be more objective than you can. Your coach can show you things you've never considered, expose your blind spots, and help you implement the powerful pivot strategies you've learned in this book.

If you've been an employee for most of your life, you'll especially appreciate the level of accountability that a coach brings to the changes you're trying to make. If your pivot is to start a business, for example, it can be difficult to build new habits and make progress without someone to hold you to your goals.

Who will ensure that you finish the five hundred words a day you need to write in order to complete your novel?

Who will hold you to the deadline for the app you're building each evening?

Who will tell you the truth about your progress on your business plan?

A coach can do all those things and more.

Your Growth Plan

Whatever proportion of time, money, or emotion you choose to invest, and wherever you choose to invest it, it's important to have a plan.

Just like investing for your financial future, your growth future needs to take a priority position. We can take a lesson from the pay-yourself-first mantra of financial planning and do the same for your growth plan.

- **Schedule your growth,** just as you'd schedule a retirement fund payment. Create the time in your calendar. Make reading time, coaching time, and training time priorities.
- **Direct your resources,** just as you would in planning your finances. If you don't set money aside for growth, it won't be there when you need it.
- **Balance your investment of time, money, and emotions.** Pivoting will almost certainly require all three.

▶● PIVOT POINT: **Growth requires a plan.**

Pivotability

I've pivoted many times. I have owned and been part of a multi-state law practice, a title insurance company, a commercial real estate investment firm, a restaurant, an Internet start-up, and a personal development seminar company. Some reinventions were small, others were more all-encompassing, but each was a pivot in its own right.

Your pivot, like mine, will probably be built from many smaller pivots. The path from corporate IT manager to entrepreneur, for example, isn't one step; it's many. It's a series of small pivots that stack up to one life-changing reinvention. The road from full-time teacher to choreographer doesn't happen with one decision but with many.

You can think of each shift, each step, each decision, as building your capacity for one single master skill: *pivotability*—the willingness to change, in the face of uncertainty, the current course of your life.

> ▶● PIVOT POINT: Pivotability is the willingness to change, in the face of uncertainty, the current course of your life.

Pivotability is just growth packaged in the form of life change. Every time you pivot a little, you grow a little. Every time you grow a little, you build the capacity to pivot a little. And through it all, you gain momentum. You learn a little, progress a little more. With each bit of growth, you add more energy to the flywheel of momentum, causing it to spin faster.

With time, you develop pivotability into a huge muscle that you can bring to bear on the most fundamental building blocks of your life—your health, your relationships, your work—to align them with your purpose. It's all possible, simply by deciding that to pivot is also to grow. *Every single person who pivots grows.*

In the same way, the reverse is true: Every time you grow a little, you pivot a little. It means that every effort you make to grow builds momentum in your pivot.

When in Doubt, Grow

After a near-fatal car accident at the age of nineteen, Brendon Burchard learned that when we're faced with the end of our lives, we ask ourselves what he calls life's last three questions: *Did I live? Did I love?* and *Did I matter?*

Brendon has been affiliated with Peaks since 2010. He is a motivational speaker and the bestselling author of *Life's Golden Ticket* and *The Charge*, and it has been wonderful to have him aligned with us in our mission to help people discover their purpose.

The great Jim Rohn once said, "Your level of success will rarely exceed your level of personal development," and Brendon is a testament to the truth of Jim's words. As Brendon told Larry King, "I don't believe in goal-based coaching, which is 'What do you want to accomplish tomorrow?' I'm more interested in 'Who do you want to become?'"

Who do *you* want to become?

Sure, improving your life is a compelling motive. Almost everyone can envision a bigger home. A better car. More money. Bigger muscles. But, as Brendon knows, when you focus only on those things, you're missing the most important distinguishing feature of people who have long, happy, successful lives: *a focus on personal development.*

I teach our students the acronym CANSI, which stands for Constant And Never-ending Self-Improvement. It's a reminder that behind every successful pivot is a choice to keep *growing*. Don't know what to do next? *Grow.* Feeling stuck? *Grow.* Experienced a setback? *Grow.* There's no downside. As Teawna Pinard said of her pivot, "I didn't really have a plan. I just knew I had to keep developing myself."

▶● PIVOT POINT: **When in doubt, *grow*.**

▶•PIVOT POINTS

> To pivot is to grow.

> The more you grow, the faster you build momentum.

> Money is a growth multiplier.

> Sometimes the investment you least *want* to make is the one you most *need* to make.

> Growth requires a plan.

> Pivotability is the willingness to change, in the face of uncertainty, the current course of your life.

> When in doubt, *grow*.

▶•PIVOTAL QUESTIONS

1. How many books did you read last year?

2. When was the last time you took a course or participated in a training program?

3. How much are you willing to invest, per month, in your personal development?

12

Pivot

The only thing worse than starting something and failing . . . is not starting something.

—SETH GODIN, ENTREPRENEUR,
AUTHOR, AND PUBLIC SPEAKER

IN 1952, Florence Chadwick stepped into the chilly waters of Catalina Island, off the shore of California, and began to swim.

Florence was no stranger to swimming. She'd started young and flourished in the sport of distance swimming, becoming the first child to swim the San Diego Bay Channel and a record holder both for swimming the English Channel and for being the first woman to swim the Channel in both directions.

Now she'd set her sights on an even greater challenge.

Her goal that day was the California coast, some twenty-six miles to the east. In between were many of the typical challenges of distance swimmers: frigid waters, sharks, currents, wind, and waves.

Fifteen hours into the swim, she was struggling. She'd battled nausea and increasing humidity, and now a thick fog had settled over the water, growing denser as the minutes passed. Soon she could see nothing but a thick wall of mist. It was then that she did something she'd never done before: She quit. She asked her team to pull her from the ocean.

Florence Chadwick's Catalina crossing was over.

◆

Change can be exhausting. If change were easy, everyone would do it. But everyone doesn't. Most people never start, and even if they do, they often give up. Like Florence, they ask to be pulled from the water, tired and unwilling to continue.

But more than anything, people often quit because they're uncertain. Like the fog that settled around Florence Chadwick, the nature of change is that you can't always know how far you are from your goal. And sometimes not knowing makes the goal seem impossibly far away.

When Florence was pulled from the water that day, she discovered a short time later that she was less than half a mile from land. Just half a mile. She later told reporters that she'd quit because she couldn't see the shore. If she had been able to, she told them, she might have made it.

Florence didn't quit because she couldn't do it. She quit because she couldn't see her goal.

Like Florence, you have a long path ahead. There will be unexpected events that fog your vision despite your best efforts to find clarity. There may be winds of change and the pull of the tides of the status quo that threaten to slow your momentum to an agonizing crawl.

And there will almost certainly be times you're afraid. Not the sharp, sudden fear of a rogue wave or a shark in the deep, but the inexorable, heavy anxiety of not knowing what's next. The anchorlike drag of doubt and uncertainty.

During such times, the temptation to quit can be overwhelming. To just give in to the doubt, the fear, the naysayers, and the uncertainty. To return to the apparent safety of how things have always been. Because when you can't see the future, it can seem, as it did to Florence Chadwick, that it's just too far away.

But know this: *You cannot pivot if you quit*. Even if you fail, you must not quit.

Because to quit is to drown. It's to suffocate in the pain of knowing that in the end you did not live the way you knew you could. To quit, then, is to *regret*.

And, like Florence, you may be closer than you think. Your goal could be just out of sight, hiding behind whatever's obscuring your vision in the present.

Two months later Florence Chadwick returned to Catalina Island and began to swim. This time when the fog set in, she kept a mental image of the coast—her goal—in her mind. When she reached the shore, not only had she become the first woman ever to complete the swim, but she'd beaten the men's record by two hours.

The Greatest Gamble

It's easy to see big goals as big risks. Swim for miles and miles through the ocean like Florence Chadwick? Too risky, you might think. Start a business in midlife? Too risky.

That's the tempting response to a dream that keeps knocking at the door of your heart—to see it as perilous. Dangerous. To see pivoting as a gamble and say, *That's not me*.

It may be time to see things differently.

First, the I'm-not-a-risk-taker story is just that: a story. It's what we tell ourselves when we're afraid to step up and claim a future that we know can be ours. Sometimes "I'm not a risk taker" is just another way of saying "I'm afraid."

Second, you *are* a risk taker. Because right now you *are* gambling. You *are* taking a risk. You're betting everything—your *life*—on the idea that you can do what you want *later*. You think that you can spend your whole life not doing what you want, assuming you can buy the freedom to do it later. You're just going to "put your head down" until the day comes when you'll have the time and money to . . .

Learn to paint, like you always dreamed.

Start a retail store, like you always dreamed.

Write the book you always wanted to.

Restore the old car you never had as a teenager.

Hike the Alps, like you always wanted to.

Volunteer your time or start a charity.

Spend a year in Italy. Or France. Or Bora Bora.

You've read this far. Let me repay your dedication by being honest: *That day isn't coming.*

Right now you're betting everything on a future that likely doesn't exist.

Does that sound like a gamble? It does to me.

It's Time to Lead

In the early days of my pivot, when I was still a Peaks student, I attended Enlightened Warrior Camp, a multiday training event.

We were completing an exercise, and a number of people from the class were leading the activity. A woman came up to me, squared off in front of me, and cocked her head.

"Why," she asked, "aren't you leading?"

I didn't even know the woman's name. We'd only started the program the day before, and I hadn't said a word.

She persisted. "You're a leader," she said. "Why aren't you leading?"

That moment was like an assault on my heart. A voice inside me asked, *Why are you playing so small in your life? What are you afraid of?*

It was a pivotal moment. From that incident on, I led in that camp. It not only transformed my experience of that week but also kick-started my path to becoming a trainer with the company.

You may not need to face off against a well-meaning yet oddly confrontational stranger to pivot, but the same principle that applied to me applies to you as well: *If you want to pivot, you need to become a leader.*

Leader is a loaded term for many people. It conjures up images of charismatic men and women giving speeches, leading charges. We almost always associate leaders with extroversion and with inspiring others to follow them.

But that's not what leadership really is, at least not for your pivot. You don't need to run a multinational company to be a leader. You don't have to lead the charge into battle, give great speeches, or inspire the troops.

But you do have to inspire yourself.

The leadership that matters for your pivot is the ability to lead *yourself*. To take charge of your life. To be responsible for your own growth. To encourage yourself to take small steps and to face your fears. And to pat yourself on the back when you win, no matter how small that win may be.

On Becoming a Hero: A Final Word

There are heroes everywhere.

We see them on the news. We read books about them and watch movies starring them. We share their stories.

Whether it's a larger-than-life hero, such as Gandhi, or the guy who left the job he hated and thrives in his own small business, there are heroes everywhere. Heroes are real, and they're a part of every culture in every country through all of history.

They all have one thing in common: *They are heroes because they live the life they dream.*

A fundamental part of the hero's journey, a term coined by Joseph Campbell, is to go from the known to the unknown. It's about leaving the safe world that the hero knows and venturing to something new and unknown. A place to be tested. Think of Luke Skywalker leaving the farm. Bilbo Baggins leaving the Shire. Neo leaving the Matrix. They all left a comfortable, known, but ultimately unfulfilling "normal" life to find themselves and eventually to become heroes.

You don't need to slay dragons or leave the planet to pivot. But there's probably no better way to capture the essence of what it means to reinvent yourself.

To pivot, you'll have to explore the unknown. I won't ask you to burn your ships or face a dragon. But you may have to leave some of your comfortable routines and predictable patterns.

And in return?

You get to become a hero of your own life. And I believe that, deep inside, that's what we all want. Because, deep down, we all know this truth: *The only thing stopping you from changing your life is you.*

The hero in this story is *you*. It's your journey. No one can take it from you or do it for you. To pivot, you need to become the hero of your own life.

Because if you can pivot—if you can change your life and live your dreams . . .

. . . what *can't* you do?

TAKING ACTION:
YOUR 21-DAY PIVOT PLAN

Motivation is what gets you started. Habit is what keeps you going.

—JIM ROHN

ANCIENT WISDOM holds that it takes twenty-one days to create a new habit.

In truth, every habit is different, every person unique, every change its own challenge. But in our experience, twenty-one days is enough time to gain an enormous amount of clarity and to build substantial momentum.

The exercises in the pages that follow aren't in random order. They're designed to help you progress at a pace—both logistical and emotional—that allows you to start small but build momentum. Remember: As long as you can keep taking the next step, you'll eventually pivot.

This is *your* pivot. Some of the steps you might repeat many times. Others you might do once. You may change the sequence or focus more on some areas than others. It's up to you.

But I will ask that you make a conscious effort to be careful of the three most dangerous words in the English language: *I know that.*

Those words are your worst enemy. They come from a place of

false confidence—in essence, from a place of fear. As soon as your conditioned mind says, *I know that*, the shades go down on your ability to learn and grow. And that's when the sun sets on your pivot, too.

"I know that" is what makes you skip exercises. It's what makes you do just part of an exercise or perhaps not write something down (*I'll just do it in my head*) when the exercise calls for writing.

My suggestion is that unless you know or discover otherwise, it's best just to follow the path in the following pages. To help you stay on track and plot your progress, I have created a 21-Day Pivot Plan Journal and a short video to get you started each day. Visit www.pivotbook.com to download the journal or complete it online. You can even sign up to receive a morning reminder by e-mail or text.

DAY 1: Create a Morning Ritual

Your pivot starts when your day does: each morning. Today's exercise is to begin to create the "space"—both physical and mental—to begin the work of pivoting.

1. Find a place in your home that can be your pivot "home base." It can be an office or spare room, or it can be as modest as a card table in a corner.
2. Make the space your own. Place there the things you'll need—this book, your journal, and any inspirational items that resonate with you.
3. Choose a consistent time each day—for most people, it's the morning—that you can dedicate to work on your pivot. Allow yourself at least thirty uninterrupted minutes. Choose carefully: This time is going to be sacred.
4. Schedule this time each day, in advance, in your calendar. Set your alarm clock if required. Make any logistical

changes to your life that you need to in order to create, and protect, this time for *you*.

5. Create your own Code of Conduct to use each morning, as outlined in Chapter 8.

> The quality of your life is equal to the quality of your rituals.
> —ADAM MARKEL

DAY 2: The Last Walk

Take twenty to thirty minutes of uninterrupted time to take a walk—alone. On the walk, imagine that these moments are *all you have left on this earth*. There are no phone calls to make, no e-mails to return or check, no people to see or speak to, no obligations or responsibilities of any kind. The only thing for you to do is to *be*—to think about your life and its meaning, what might come next, or anything else that comes to mind.

The idea is to take this exercise seriously and fully believe that your life will end when the thirty minutes have passed. See what you see, feel what you feel, experience what you experience, and when your time is up (literally and figuratively), spend a few minutes in quiet contemplation of what the exercise was like for you. Write down the perceptions that you have gained.

> A miracle is the breakthrough that occurs when we shift
> our perception of a situation. Therefore, a "miracle"
> can be a mere change in consciousness.
> —MARIANNE WILLIAMSON

DAY 3: Meditation

Today, spend just five minutes in quiet meditation.

Remember that meditation is simply a quieting of the mind. It is mindfulness. You don't have to take a class or read a book to learn how to meditate. When you practice, just allow your mind to do whatever it wants without judgment, and then gently guide it back to a place of stillness. Meditation is a training; it is a gentle discipline.

1. Choose a quiet place where you won't be disturbed.
2. Sit comfortably. You can sit on the floor, on a cushion, or in a chair—just choose a comfortable seated position and try to keep your back straight.
3. Gently close your eyes and turn your attention to your breath.
4. Breathe naturally, and be aware of the sensation of your breath entering and leaving your nostrils.
5. As your mind wanders, gently guide it back to your breath. At first you may find this very difficult and feel as if your mind is busy or racing. Don't worry. That's normal. The more you practice, the easier it will become to find stillness and silence.

Add this gentle discipline to your morning ritual. Do it for five minutes each day, and when you feel comfortable, increase it by a minute or two until you can comfortably do it for fifteen minutes or longer.

> Do not dwell in the past, do not dream of the future,
> concentrate the mind on the present moment.
> —BUDDHA

DAY 4: Timeline Exercise

Create a timeline of your life working backward from your last day.

This exercise is different from imagining a point in the future. In this exercise, you're focused on specific results and working your way backward, accomplishment by accomplishment, milestone by milestone, until you reach the present.

Consider the following:

- What results/accomplishments would be nonnegotiable?
- What experiences would be a must?
- What wisdom would you have gained?
- What legacy would you leave?
- What people or causes would you have served?
- What relationships would you have established?
- Whose lives would be better because you have lived?

Aim for a minimum of twenty milestones in your timeline.

Bonus exercise: Write your own eulogy based on the answers to the questions above.

Reminder: Visit www.pivotbook.com to download your Pivot Plan Journal or to complete your exercises online.

> Life isn't about finding yourself. Life is about creating yourself.
> —GEORGE BERNARD SHAW

DAY 5: Beliefs That Resonate

Creating a new life requires believing new things. After all, what you've believed so far has brought you to where you are.

Below is a list of the beliefs and ways of thinking and being that have helped me and countless thousands of others positively transform their lives.

Go through the list twice.

In the first pass, simply identify the ways of thinking and being that immediately resonate with you. This list is not exhaustive, so feel free to add your own.

In the next pass, mark the ten that resonate with you the most.

Write your ten beliefs in your 21-Day Pivot Plan Journal.

You can begin to adopt these new beliefs immediately by saying them out loud—declaring them to the Universe and sending out your vibration of energy into the ether—at least once every day for the next twenty-one days.

1. "I expect and receive miracles."
2. "I think 'both' rather than 'either/or.'"
3. "I focus on what I want, not what I don't want."
4. "What I focus on expands."
5. "I am worthy and deserving to receive."
6. "I have a big *why*."
7. "I am a divine being with a divine purpose."
8. "I have important gifts to share in the world."
9. "I add value in the world."
10. "I am guided by infinite intelligence."
11. "I am a money magnet."
12. "There are no problems, only opportunities to grow."
13. "I can handle any challenge when and if it arises."
14. "I am enough."
15. "I prefer sloppy success over perfect mediocrity."
16. "There is more than enough for everyone."
17. "My thoughts become things."
18. "I just get one done!"
19. "I take successful baby steps."
20. "I am always moving forward."
21. "I make the right decision."

22. "I bless that which I want."
23. "The more people I serve, the richer I am."
24. "The more solutions I create, the richer I am."
25. "I can do anything."
26. "I never blame, justify, or complain."
27. "I am willing to do what is hard."
28. "My word is law in the Universe."
29. "I am the eye of the storm."
30. "Out of chaos comes order."
31. "I am comfortable with chaos, ambiguity, and the unknown."
32. "I love my life."
33. "I am the master of my fate and the captain of my soul."
34. "I am a W.I.T. person."
35. "I succeed with grace, elegance, and ease."
36. "I create my life."
37. "I earn money when I sleep, when I play, and even when I am on vacation."
38. "I am a teacher. I have important information to share."
39. "Either I am growing or I am dying."
40. "I acknowledge and celebrate my successes."
41. "I complete what I start."
42. "How I do anything is how I do everything."
43. "Nothing has meaning except for the meaning I give it."
44. "I manifest the glory of God that is within me."
45. "I am powerful beyond measure."
46. "Om na ma ha—it's not about me."
47. "My highest desires are manifesting now."
48. "I have complete faith in myself and in God sufficient to achieve the manifestations of whatever my heart desires."
49. "I follow my heart. My heart has only answers."
50. "I see all change as being in my highest interest."
51. "I am curious about all that is happening in my life."
52. "I stay in the present, here and now."
53. "I live with passion."

54. "The quality of my life is equal to the quality of my rituals."
55. "There is no try. I do or do not do!"
56. "I take massive action."
57. "I am decisive."
58. "I live without attachment."
59. "I let go of anger and resentment easily and quickly."
60. "I think big."
61. "My money works hard for me."
62. "I am excellent at managing my money."
63. "I am excellent at managing my energy."
64. "I love promoting my value to the world."
65. "I get paid based on the value I provide."
66. "I act in spite of fear, doubt, or worry."
67. "I am a child of God, and I can only meet with the pure expressions of God."
68. "I forgive myself and others easily."

What matters is not the idea a man holds,
but the depth at which he holds it.
—EZRA POUND

DAY 6: Mental Diet Day

Today, try Emmet Fox's mental diet idea from Chapter 5 for just a single day. Try not to hold, dwell on, or sustain any negative thoughts. They will naturally arise out of habit, but that's okay as long as you don't sustain them. Likewise, don't speak anything negative, either. Here's a reminder from Mr. Fox of just how important this is:

"What you think upon grows. Whatever you allow to occupy your mind you magnify in your life. Whether the subject of your thought be good or bad, the law works and the condition grows. Any subject that you keep out of your mind tends to diminish in your life, because what you do not use atrophies. The more you think of grievances, the more such trials you will continue to receive; the more you think of the good fortune you have had, the more good fortune will come to you."

> We don't see things as they are, we see them as we are.
> —ANAÏS NIN, *SEDUCTION OF THE MINOTAUR*

DAY 7: A Letter from Your Future Self

Imagine that it's ten years from now and your life is as you always wished it could be. The things you've envisioned and hoped have come to pass. The great things you always wanted to do—you've done them or are on your way to doing them.

Write a one-page letter from that place in the future. What will you tell your current self about what life is like? What advice will you give yourself? What encouragement?

> Be of good cheer. The future is as bright as your faith.
> —THOMAS S. MONSON, PRESIDENT OF THE CHURCH
> OF JESUS CHRIST OF LATTER-DAY SAINTS

DAY 8: Emotional Awareness

Today's task is to become aware of the emotions you have connected to your dreams, your past, your fears, and the idea of change. Answer the following ten questions.

1. In what three specific areas of your life could you reevaluate your situation based on what you know today versus what you knew in the past?
2. How could you reorganize your life so that it is more in harmony with your dreams and desires?
3. What would you most like to spend your time doing?
4. What would you do if you knew you could not fail?
5. What would other people think if you quit your job or shut down your business?
6. What is your greatest fear?
7. How have you handled change in the past?
8. Whose approval do you need in your life?
9. What excites you?
10. What makes you feel fulfilled and useful?

> Let's not forget that the little emotions are the great captains
> of our lives and we obey them without realizing it.
> —VINCENT VAN GOGH

DAY 9: Face a Fear

Today's task is small but challenging. Your job is to take a small action that makes you uncomfortable, or a little afraid, when you think of it. You don't need to go skydiving or be reckless.

For example, you might:

- Approach a stranger and ask for the time or directions.
- Tell someone close that you love him or her.
- Broach a difficult subject with a coworker, friend, or boss. You might want to discuss a raise, a disappointment, or a personal conflict.

- Apologize sincerely to someone you've wronged.
- Add up all your debt, if you have any, to one sum.

The goal is simply to do one small thing that makes you uncomfortable.

> Everything you want is on the other side of fear.
> —JACK CANFIELD, COAUTHOR OF THE
> *CHICKEN SOUP FOR THE SOUL* SERIES

DAY 10: Release the Past

For this clearing exercise you may wish to find a private place to sit where you might also make loud sounds if necessary.

In Chapter 2, I gave you several statements to complete, designed to identify negative emotions from the past that may be holding you back. Choose three emotional issues that came up during that process and commit those issues to memory. For example, "I am angry at myself for staying in a job that I can't stand for the last twenty years, and now I feel stuck."

Now bring up the first emotional issue or feeling. Get in touch with how it makes you feel. Feel the feeling in your body. If you can touch this area of your body with your hand, touch it now. Let the feeling of that emotion or issue grow in strength; really feel the emotion deep inside you.

Now answer the following questions quietly but out loud:

- Do I like feeling this way?
- Do I want to let it go?
- Am I willing to let it go?
- When am I willing to let it go?

If you are willing to let this emotional issue go now, say out loud, "I am willing to let [whatever the emotional issue is] go now." Say the full sentence.

Now take a deep breath, and let it go with a sound!

Take a deep breath, and let it go with a sound!!

Take a deep breath, and let it go with a sound!!!

Shake out your hands and your body and smile. If you are unwilling to let it go now, just be open to releasing it at some time in the future.

Follow the same process for each of your three emotional issues. If you were unwilling to let one of the issues go, or if you're unsure if it cleared, or to make doubly sure, bring that issue up again now.

Feel it, feel where you feel it, touch it (it might have moved). Make the feeling of that emotion even stronger. Ask yourself:

- What does this feeling or issue do for me?
- What's my payoff for having it?
- Does it protect me and support me now?
- Does it help anyone else?
- Do I really still need it now?
- What's the use of having it now?
- What will happen if I let it go? Who would I be, what would I be like, if I let it go?

Now answer the original four questions again quietly but out loud:

- Do I like feeling this way?
- Do I want to let it go?
- Am I willing to let it go?
- When am I willing to let it go?

If you are willing to let it go now, say to yourself, "I am willing to let [whatever the emotional issue is] go now." Say the full sentence out loud. Say it again. Say it again! If you're not willing, just be open to the possibility of not giving it any more of your precious energy and allowing it to wither away on its own.

Know that you've now taken a heavy load off of your shoulders and out of your body. Take a big, deep breath and let it out with a sound. Again. And again. Feel the sense of freedom. Feel the presence of lightness. Feel the emptiness. This is good. Now fill this emptiness with love and with light.

Put one hand on your heart and one hand on your belly. Feel love for those you are closest to and for all of your brothers and sisters sharing this planet with you at this time. Feel love for Mother Earth, recognizing how she's always there supporting you. Feel love for the Universe or Spirit and appreciation for the life you've been given. And feel complete and unconditional love for yourself. Just take your arms, put them around you, and give yourself a big, loving hug.

Feel unwavering and total self-acceptance of who you are at this time and your willingness to learn and grow. Make the decision to love yourself fully as you are right now. Put your hands down. Breathe in and let the breath out with a smile, for you've now been given a fresh, new start. You now have a totally clean slate.

To go even more deeply, you can read the book *The Sedona Method*, which this process is based on, or attend a Millionaire Mind Intensive program almost any weekend of the year somewhere around the world.

> In the process of letting go you will lose many things
> from the past, but you will find yourself.
> —DEEPAK CHOPRA

DAY 11: Forgive

Forgiveness is the balm that soothes the most stinging sore. Forgiveness is the miraculous cure for what ails most people on the inside.

Without forgiveness we tend to deteriorate, because the cells of our body carry the poisons of anger, resentment, condemnation, judgment, and jealousy. All this is unnecessary.

Sit on a chair in a comfortable position with your legs uncrossed and your palms facing up. Take three slow, deep breaths . . . in and out . . . breathe in and out . . . again deeply in through the nose and out through the mouth.

Now imagine that a person you have been angry with is sitting in front of you. See him or her looking into your eyes. Imagine him or her saying these words: "I am sorry for hurting you. I never intended to do so. I did the best I could at the time. I never would have done what I did if I had known it would cause you so much pain."

Make the picture of this scene in full living color as if it were happening right now. Imagine yourself leaning over and hugging or at least shaking hands with this person in forgiveness, knowing that everyone always does the best they can at the time, including you.

Feel the negative energy leaving you now. Feel the lightness and the freedom in your body as peace and harmony are restored inside of you.

I urge you to complete the process with the person in your visualization. Whether it means saying "I forgive you" or "I'm angry with you" or "I love you," it's important to say things while you can. If the person in your visualization has passed on, you can write a letter and burn it in a ceremony or write an e-mail and send it or delete it. The choice is yours, but remember that this process is not about the other person; it's for and about *you*.

As with the letting go process yesterday, to heal your past relationships at an even deeper level, consider attending an MMI program this year. See the resource guide at the end of this plan for more information.

All forgiveness is a gift to yourself.
—DR. HELEN SCHUCMAN, *A COURSE IN MIRACLES*

DAY 12: Draft Your Vision

In this exercise, you will start to create a draft vision for your life today. Start with the phrase "My vision is . . ." and then write what you would like to see yourself accomplishing in the world from today forward.

Let the words flow from your sense of mission and purpose, your sense of calling. Allow the words to flow without interference from the little voice inside your head, which has the habit of posing what-ifs and reasons why things won't be possible.

Simply write what you want and intend to be true, without including limitations of any kind. Do not allow your protective, conditioned mind to let you play small during this exercise. In fact, do the opposite: See how big you can still dream.

If you want to be an author, why not be a *New York Times* number one bestselling author? If you love dance, why not dance professionally and be paid handsomely for it? Why not own a yoga retreat or a studio to teach art to kids or seniors? Why not open a rescue ranch for unwanted animals?

Whatever your heart's desire is, speak it to yourself. Take no more than ten to fifteen minutes.

> A vision is not just a picture of what could be; it is an appeal to our better selves, a call to become something more.
> —ROSABETH MOSS KANTER, ERNEST L. ARBUCKLE PROFESSOR
> OF BUSINESS ADMINISTRATION, HARVARD BUSINESS SCHOOL

DAY 13: Create a Mantra

I have a sticky note from several years ago on which I wrote, "Adam Markel, CEO of New Peaks." I was a trainer at the time I wrote that, and I used it as a mantra. Within a short time, I became CEO, just as my mantra predicted. Then, about a year and a half later, I was demoted.

One summer I was at our house on Martha's Vineyard. We keep an old Mercedes station wagon there—there are more than 117,000 miles on Bessie and she's still chugging along. One day I got into the car and noticed that the little yellow sticky note with the mantra "Adam Markel, CEO of New Peaks" was still on the dashboard. In that moment I had a choice: I could take the sticky note down, or I could leave it on Bessie's dash. I decided to leave it, thinking, *This will be true someday. I'm not giving up.*

Not even a year later, I was reinstated to the position of CEO at New Peaks.

There is power in creating mantras, however short, however simple, that reveal things about us that the world doesn't see yet.

What single sentence can you create that would inspire you daily and capture your vision? Write a draft of that sentence now, and include it as a mantra in your morning ritual. Don't be stuck trying to make it perfect. Just write.

> All you need is already within you.
> —NISARGADATTA MAHARAJ, INDIAN PHILOSOPHER

DAY 14: Establish an Evening Ritual

In addition to the morning ritual, this one simple evening practice has been proven to increase happiness, and it takes just a few moments a day.

Each night before bed, write down three things that you are grateful for.

The first two are for things that happened during that day. These gratitude statements can be as simple or as involved as you like—

whatever works with your schedule. You might write that you are grateful for the meal you shared with your family at dinner, how the sunshine warmed your face during your lunch hour, or how you felt when you read a bedtime story to your daughter. The idea is just to write two things, so the exercise can be done quite quickly before going to sleep.

The third statement of gratitude will be for something that has yet to occur in your life but that you wish to have happen in the near future. You might want to give thanks in advance for the fact that you found your dream home, or that your loan to buy your home was approved, or that you found an agent to represent the sale of your book.

> He is a wise man who does not grieve for the things which
> he has not, but rejoices for those which he has.
> —EPICTETUS

DAY 15: Baby-Step Brainstorm

Based on your pivot vision, take fifteen minutes to brainstorm a list of steps that you imagine you might have to take in the initial weeks of your reinvention.

- Focus on the first few weeks or month of change.
- Don't worry about sequence or details, just write.
- Make the steps as small and doable as possible.

Once you have a list, ask yourself these three questions:

- What would be the very first step I need to take?
- Am I willing to take it?
- When?

> Faith is taking the first step, even when you
> don't see the whole staircase.
> —MARTIN LUTHER KING JR.

DAY 16: Try It On

Who do you know who has already done what you're trying to do? If no one comes to mind, make a commitment to ask five other people if *they* know someone. (Tip: You can broaden your reach considerably if you put your request out using social media.)

Contact that person and ask if you can spend a short time with him or her to get some advice on how he or she did it.

> All life is an experiment. The more experiments you make the better.
> —RALPH WALDO EMERSON

DAY 17: Identify Your Stakeholders

A stakeholder is someone who stands to gain if you successfully pivot, or stands to lose if you don't. That means immediate family and dependents, investors, partners, and possibly close friends.

Who are your stakeholders? Make a list of the people you believe fit the criteria.

Now schedule a time to meet with each of them.

> What we once enjoyed and deeply loved we can never
> lose, for all that we love deeply becomes a part of us.
> —HELEN KELLER

DAY 18: Find a Mentor

Revisit Chapter 9, "Pivot People," and the section on mentors.

Based on your pivot vision so far, who do you know, or know of, who might have wisdom to offer? Try to list three names.

If you're starting a business, for example, you might contact a successful entrepreneur. If you're changing careers, contact someone with a similar job or someone at a company you aspire to work for in order to gain insight into what helped them make their company work. If you want to write a book, talk to someone else who's published one.

Contact people who know what they're doing, and ask if you can spend a few minutes with them to get some advice on your pivot.

> There is no lack of knowledge out there . . .
> Just a shortage of asking for help.
> —MARK J. CARTER, MARKETER AND ENTREPRENEUR

DAY 19: Start a Mastermind

Just as it takes a whole orchestra to play a symphony, it takes more than one person to create a new life.

Create a list of at least six people you think would make excellent collaborators. Review the section on peers in Chapter 9 for tips.

Once you've created your list, contact each person and invite them to join your mastermind group.

(Bonus: To read more about the power and influence of the mastermind, I recommend the 1937 classic *Think and Grow Rich* by Napoleon Hill.)

Individually, we are one drop. Together, we are an ocean.
—RYUNOSUKE SATORO, JAPANESE WRITER

DAY 20: Attend a Training Workshop or Seminar

I didn't attend a personal growth training seminar until I was past forty, but my life changed profoundly when I did. What I quickly discovered was that attending a great seminar is one of the most powerful ways not only to raise your energy and develop your skills but to meet other people who are on a similar journey.

There are many choices, but the most important one by far is simply to begin where you are right now. I began my own pivot journey when I attended an MMI event in New Jersey. I have now witnessed the transformation of people's lives weekend after weekend. You can get started at www.newpeaks.com, and see the special complimentary tuition certificate for you and a guest to attend a Reignite Live weekend (your "Golden Ticket") at the end of this plan. You can also check the resource guide for more great choices.

The best time to plant a tree is twenty years
ago. The second best time is now.
—CHINESE PROVERB

DAY 21: Hire a Coach

I believe in the power of humility. When you acknowledge your own shortcomings and areas in which you need to improve, you open new doors and remove obstacles.

A coach is someone who can help you do this and more. A coach can be more objective than you can. Your coach can show you things you've never considered, expose your blind spots, and help you implement the powerful pivot strategies you have learned in this book.

You can find a list of coaches at the end of this guide.

> When you talk, you are only repeating what you already
> know. But if you listen, you may learn something new.
> —J. P. McEVOY, AMERICAN WRITER

DAY 22 AND BEYOND: Take Action

The Law of Inertia states that a body at rest tends to stay at rest, and a body in motion tends to stay in motion. The most important thing for you to do now is to stay in motion. Stay active in your new practices and reignited mind-set. Decide today what book you are going to read next. Go online and find a great course or program to enroll in. Keep your new rituals each day, starting with what you think and do when you first wake up in the morning. Here's the ritual I use each and every day when my feet hit the floor: I take a deep breath and a healthy pause to give thanks for all that I have to be grateful for, and then I say out loud, "I love my life!" Try it on and see how it feels for you. After all, you have nothing to lose and everything to gain, so take action! One thing is certain, and that is that nothing much will ever change in your life unless you are willing and able to take action, and do so over and over again.

Nothing in your life is going to change by itself, no matter how often you visualize it, affirm it, or wish it to be true. You must take action.

In the days ahead, you can keep your pivot in motion by simply doing these three things:

1. Continue your morning ritual. Consider including elements of movement, such as a walk or workout, and meditation. Refine your ritual over time. You might include reading, study, planning, and more.
2. Ask yourself the key pivot question: *Am I willing to take the next step?*
3. If the answer is yes, then *take it.*

As the saying goes: Pray, but move your feet! All of the Universe will come to your aid when you take the first step.

Lastly, and most important, remember who you are in all that you are doing. You are a divine being who was brought to this earth to make manifest the glory that is within you. You were born for a very important reason and purpose, and it is part of your life's journey to explore the infinite growth potential within yourself. You are, as Marianne Williamson reminds you, beautiful, talented, fabulous, and intended for greatness. Keep in mind that there are no straight lines in the Universe. There are many points along the way where you will have the creative opportunity to pivot and find new *chi* (energy) to go even further. I wish you every Blessing along your path.

Until we meet again . . .

RESOURCE GUIDE

Books

Secrets of the Millionaire Mind by T. Harv Eker

The Road Less Traveled by M. Scott Peck

The Sedona Method by Hale Dwoskin

Awaken the Giant Within by Anthony Robbins

Think and Grow Rich by Napoleon Hill

The Untethered Soul by Michael A. Singer

Don't Sweat the Small Stuff by Michael Mantell

The Seven Day Mental Diet by Emmet Fox

The Power of Now by Eckhart Tolle

The Alchemist by Paulo Coelho

Karmic Management by Geshe Michael Roach and Lama Christie McNally

The Other F Word by Juliana Ericson

Start with Why by Simon Sinek

The Seven Spiritual Laws of Success by Deepak Chopra

Autobiography of a Yogi by Paramahansa Yogananda

Delivering Happiness by Tony Hsieh

Rich Dad Poor Dad by Robert Kiyosaki with Sharon Lechter

Outwitting the Devil by Napoleon Hill

Redemption by Berny Dohrmann

The Holographic Universe by Michael Dooley

Jonathan Livingston Seagull by Richard Bach

Coaching

New Peaks: www.newpeaks.com/programs/coaching

Tony Robbins: www.tonyrobbins.com

Vistage (leadership and business coaching for executives): www.vistage.com

Dream University: www.dreamuniversity.com

Lisa Nichols: www.motivatingthemasses.com

Training Courses, Workshops, and Retreats

For a full guide to all New Peaks programs, courses, camps, and retreats—including Mission Possible, NLP Mastery Intensive, Ultimate Relationship Retreat, Inner Warrior Training, The Stage Trainer Boot Camp, Master Wealth Creator, Business Incubator Revolution, Global Mastermind, and CEO Mentoring—visit www.newpeaks.com.

Tony Robbins: www.tonyrobbins.com

Brendon Burchard: www.brendonburchard.com

Greg and Tamara Montana: www.heartvirtue.com

Other

CEO Space International (business development and networking): www.ceospaceinternational.com

Calm (meditation instruction, apps, and resources): www.calm.com

---

3-Day REIGNITE Weekend

SEMINAR VOUCHER — **BONUS**

To reward you for taking the first step toward transforming your life by purchasing *Pivot*, Adam Markel and New Peaks are offering you and one guest an exclusive opportunity to attend the 3-Day Weekend Seminar as VIPs. At this world-famous program, you will uncover your inner fire for success and kick-start your purpose, power, and game plan for creating even more fulfillment and inner peace, both personally and professionally. You will change your life forever!

To download your seminar voucher
and register, visit www.reigniteweekend.com
or www.millionairemindexperience.com,
or call 1-888-868-8883, option 2.

Use promo code PIVOTBOOK when you register.

RECOMMENDED SEMINARS, COURSES, COACHING, AND CAMPS

SEMINARS

REIGNITE Weekend—3 Days
At REIGNITE, you will uncover your inner fire for success and kick-start your purpose, power, and game plan for creating even more fulfillment and inner peace, both personally and professionally. For details and schedules, please visit www.reigniteweekend.com or call 1-888-868-8883, option 2.

Millionaire Mind Experience—3 Days
The world-famous Millionaire Mind Experience Seminar will transform your financial life forever. You will learn the how-to-win-the-money game and get on the path to financial freedom and reset your "money blueprint" so that financial success is natural and automatic for you. For details and schedules, please visit www.millionairemind experience.com or call 1-888-868-8883, option 2.

COURSES

Mission Possible
If you ever wanted to own a business that creates "money with meaning," this program not only shows you how to turn your mission into millions but also certifies you to be a New Peaks coach, mentor, and mastermind facilitator. On top of that, you will learn about and receive a certification as a Neuro-Linguistic Programming Practitioner. For details and schedules, please visit www.new peaks.com or call 1-888-868-8883, option 2.

COACHING

CEO Mentoring Program
This is our premier Executive Coaching Program for professionals, business owners, and entrepreneurs. For details and schedules, please visit www.newpeaks.com or call 1-888-868-8883, option 2.

Extreme Health—3 Days
The goal for optimum health is to have a surplus of energy, strength, and power. At Extreme Health, the greatest medical and alternative health experts in the world will teach you health tactics and strategies ranging from the truth about diets and proper sleep habits, to choosing superfoods and avoiding those that sap your body's energy.

Guerrilla Business School—4 Days
At Guerrilla Business School, you will learn how to create wealth quickly in any business you choose along with how to create million-dollar ideas, street-smart financing, maverick marketing methods, real-world negotiation strategies, and much more.

Life Directions—3 Days
The objective of this program is for you to gain money with meaning. At Life Directions, you will discover your true mission in a way that is highly successful in the real world. It's an absolute must for anyone wanting clarity and focus.

Never Work Again—4 Days
Learn up to fifteen unique passive business opportunities and how to structure them to generate income without any additional work from you—forever.

Train the Trainer Certification I and II—5 Days Each
Earn $20,000 a weekend teaching what you love. That's exactly what you'll learn at Train the Trainer. Discover everything you need to be successful in the training business, including choosing the right topic, designing an incredible program, using accelerated-learning technologies, and marketing for success. By the end of this course, you will be a "hot" trainer and know exactly how to become a rich one, too. For details and schedules, please visit www.newpeaks.com or call 1-888-868-8883, option 2.

CAMPS

Enlightened Warrior Training—5 Days
The definition of *enlightened warrior* is "one who conquers oneself." In this high-intensity program, you will learn how to access your true power at will and succeed in spite of anything. By the end of Warrior Training, nothing will ever stop you again.

Wizard Training Camp—5 Days
Learn to manifest what you want with elegance and grace. At Wizard Training, you will learn to live as the "eye of the storm": calm, centered, and peaceful in spite of anything. This camp is open only to graduates of Enlightened Warrior Training.

Ultimate Relationship Retreat—5 Days
This is our signature relationship program designed to identify your relationship blueprint and set it for success. With the guidance of some of the world's leading experts, you will gain insights and direction to critically review, break down, and improve all your personal relationships. You will come away from this program using the seven pillars of the ultimate relationship with everyone you come in contact with. The Ultimate Relationship Retreat is, bar none, the most effective and transforming program. We will assess and change your relationship blueprint right on the spot!

ACKNOWLEDGMENTS

Pivot began as a guide for our children as they traveled through life. Along the way, it grew into something much more: an entire book, and a source of inspiration and practical information, for potential Pivoters everywhere.

My own experience has taught me that even small pivots in direction can create massive transformation over time, and I want to acknowledge some beautiful beings who both inspired and contributed mightily to this one.

To my wife, Randi, for her unconditional love, trust, and belief in me. To our children, Chelsea, Lindsay, Max, and Eden, who are the reflection of my soul. To my dad, who showed me what perseverance in the pursuit of great writing looks like. To my mom, who inspired in me a desire to fully express myself. To my younger brother, Keith, and sister-in-law, Zjantelle, for modeling how to pivot with style. To Alyse and Jim for their love. To Jessica, Zade, Van, Jude, and Phoenix for being beautiful bright lights in our new world. To my editor, Leslie, and agent, Francesca, for their belief in this project and in our opportunity to change many lives. To my developmental editor, Dan, for his invaluable assistance shaping the content to an even deeper level. To my dear friends and business partners Richard and Veronica for their faith in me.

And last, but certainly not least: to the Pivoters who shared their stories of personal and professional reinvention, which will inspire generations of people to take action!

INDEX

pervasiveness, of setbacks, 179

pessimism, 178–79

physics, of momentum, 115, 116, 116n

Pinard, Teawna:

  and Big-D decision, 102–3, 104, 106, 107, 108

  and growth, 205

  and perseverance, 188–89

  and rituals, 145–46

pivotability, and growth, 203–4

pivotal habits, 140, 141–42

Pivotal Questions:

  baby steps, 134

  beliefs, 24

  Big-D decision, 111

  fear, 62

  growth, 207

  identity, 81

  journal for, xxi

  letting go, 44

  life's purpose, 101

  pivot people, 174

  resilience, 191

  rituals, 155

pivot behaviors, and momentum, xxi

pivot energy, tapping into, 60

pivoting:

  in baby steps, 121–29

  in basketball, xvi, xxii

  big-leap approach, 120, 121, 122

  and change, xxii, xxiii, 16–17, 135, 136, 152, 153, 213, 215

  as choice, 14

  costs of, 57

  definitions of, xvi

  as emotional threat, 49–50

  and fear, 46–48, 49

  and fear stories, 50–54

  and growth, 195–96

  and heroes, 212–13

  and leadership, 211–12

  as process, xviii, 37–38

  and quitting, xx, 208–10

  reinventing your life, xv–xvi, xvii, xviii–xix, xxii–xxiii

  and risk, 210–11

  as step-by-step process, 16–17, 37–39

  and vision, 84–86

  See also clarity; momentum

pivot people:

  and clarity, 159

  and collaboration, 158–59, 167–69

  curating of, 170–72

  and growth, 202

  mentors, 164–67, 198, 200

  and momentum, 117

  peers, 167–69

  Pivotal Questions, 174

  Pivot Points, 157, 159, 163, 165, 166, 167, 172, 173

  role of, 156–57

  stakeholders, 161–64, 199

  virtuous cycle of growth, 159–61

  and vision, 158–59

pivot phone booth, identity change, 6, 63–64, 75

Pivot Points:

  baby steps, 122, 125, 127, 128, 129, 133

  beliefs, 14, 15, 17, 20, 21, 23

  Big-D decision, 104, 107, 108, 109, 110

  clarity level, 6

  fear, 47, 51, 52, 53, 54, 61

  growth, 196, 197, 199, 200, 204, 205, 206

  identity, 66, 69, 72, 74, 76, 79, 80

  letting go, 33, 37, 38, 39, 41, 43

  life's purpose, 86, 88, 90, 93, 97, 100

ABOUT THE AUTHOR

Adam Markel is a transformational teacher who inspires, empowers, and guides people to live authentically, purposefully, and powerfully from their hearts. Adam is the CEO of New Peaks LLC (formerly Peak Potentials). An international training firm, New Peaks has delivered world-class educational programs to more than one million people in over 104 countries.

Prior to his position as CEO, Adam was a senior trainer with Peak Potentials and has personally trained more than one hundred thousand people in the United States, Southeast Asia, Canada, Europe, and Australia. In addition, Adam is a keynote speaker for groups and conferences around the world, including:

Infusionsoft
American Gem Society
California Chiropractic Association
National Achievers Congress
Get Motivated

A recognized expert in the integration of business and personal transformation, Adam has been interviewed by:

Fox News
Newsday
New York Post
Wall Street Journal
Observer
Entrepreneur
Investor's Business Daily
American Express

Prior to his work with New Peaks, Adam spent eighteen years as an attorney representing clients in state and federal court in New York and New Jersey. Adam holds a law degree from St. John's University and an undergraduate degree in English from the University of Massachusetts Amherst, where he graduated magna cum laude. Adam is a former local chapter president of Business Network International in New Jersey.

He lives in Carlsbad, California, where one of his greatest joys has been raising four amazing children with Randi, his wife of more than twenty-five years.